VAUGHAN PUBLIC LIBRARIES

3 3288 10149239 7   JUN 2020

Praise for *Kubernetes Operators*

"Kubernetes has emerged as the world's most powerful container orchestration platform, but its true power is hidden behind an extensible API and automation framework that will redefine how future platforms are built and operated; this book is the missing manual."

—*Kelsey Hightower, Technologist, Google Cloud*

"The *Kubernetes Operators* book by Jason and Josh is something that should not be missing on your (digital) bookshelf, if you're serious about Kubernetes. It's hands-on, covers the why and the how, and enables you to successfully apply the operator pattern in your environment. I'd consider this book the perfect followup to *Programming Kubernetes*."

—*Michael Hausenblas, Amazon Web Services*

"This book is essential for anyone looking to adopt the Operator Paradigm for their critical workloads. It provides a comprehensive overview of design principles, implementation paths and traps, and utilization of the existing ecosystem."

—*Anish Asthana, Software Engineer, Red Hat*

"Working with Jason over the past several years, I have always wanted a dump of what's in his head, and now I have it! Josh and Jason have created an essential guide for anyone creating operators, and it will be a significant advantage for us as we look to mature our operator into the Auto Pilot phase with the goal of becoming a true 'Kubernetes Application Reliability Engineering' function for our customers."

—*Dave Meurer, Technical Global Alliances, Synopsys, Inc.*

"Another brilliant publication by Josh and Jason that provides market-leading data for Kubernetes Operators."

mes, Global Alliances, Synopsys, Inc.

D1226098

Kubernetes Operators
Automating the Container Orchestration Platform

Jason Dobies and Joshua Wood

Beijing · Boston · Farnham · Sebastopol · Tokyo

Kubernetes Operators

by Jason Dobies and Joshua Wood

Copyright © 2020 Red Hat, Inc. All rights reserved.

Published by O'Reilly Media, Inc., 1005 Gravenstein Highway North, Sebastopol, CA 95472.

O'Reilly books may be purchased for educational, business, or sales promotional use. Online editions are also available for most titles (*http://oreilly.com*). For more information, contact our corporate/institutional sales department: 800-998-9938 or *corporate@oreilly.com*.

Acquisitions Editor: John Devins	**Indexer:** Ellen Troutman-Zaig
Development Editor: Virginia Wilson	**Interior Designer:** David Futato
Production Editor: Deborah Baker	**Cover Designer:** Karen Montgomery
Copyeditor: Rachel Head	**Illustrator:** Rebecca Demarest
Proofreader: Sonia Saruba	

March 2020:   First Edition

Revision History for the First Edition

2020-01-13:   First Release
2020-02-21:   Second Release

See *http://oreilly.com/catalog/errata.csp?isbn=9781492048046* for release details.

The O'Reilly logo is a registered trademark of O'Reilly Media, Inc. *Kubernetes Operators*, the cover image, and related trade dress are trademarks of O'Reilly Media, Inc.

The views expressed in this work are those of the authors, and do not represent the publisher's views. While the publisher and the authors have used good faith efforts to ensure that the information and instructions contained in this work are accurate, the publisher and the authors disclaim all responsibility for errors or omissions, including without limitation responsibility for damages resulting from the use of or reliance on this work. Use of the information and instructions contained in this work is at your own risk. If any code samples or other technology this work contains or describes is subject to open source licenses or the intellectual property rights of others, it is your responsibility to ensure that your use thereof complies with such licenses and/or rights.

This work is part of a collaboration between O'Reilly and Red Hat, Inc. See our statement of editorial independence (*https://oreil.ly/editorial-independence*).

978-1-492-04804-6

[LSI]

To my kids, Leanne and Austin, know that it is never easy to have to tell you "No, daddy has to work." Realize that all of it—the meetings, the trips, the book—all of it is for you two. I have your backs in whatever the future holds for you, and I can't wait to see the awesome things you two do.
—Jason

To Shayna.
—Joshua

Table of Contents

Preface

Kubernetes is a popular container orchestrator. It harnesses many computers together into one large computing resource and establishes a means of addressing that resource through the Kubernetes application programming interface (API). Kubernetes is open source software with origins at Google, developed over the last five years by a large group of collaborators under the auspices of the Cloud Native Computing Foundation (CNCF) (*https://www.cncf.io/*).

An Operator extends Kubernetes to automate the management of the entire lifecycle of a particular application. Operators serve as a packaging mechanism for distributing applications on Kubernetes, and they monitor, maintain, recover, and upgrade the software they deploy.

Who This Book Is For

If you've deployed applications on a Kubernetes cluster, you'll be familiar with some of the challenges and aspirations that forged the Operator pattern. If you've maintained foundation services like databases and filesystems in their own ghetto outside your orchestrated clusters, and you yearn to bring them into the neighborhood, this guide to Kubernetes Operators is for you.

What You Will Learn

This book explains what an Operator is and how Operators extend the Kubernetes API. It shows how to deploy and use existing Operators, and how to create and distribute Operators for your applications using the Red Hat Operator Framework (*https://github.com/operator-framework*). We relate good practices for designing, building, and distributing Operators, and we explain the thinking that animates Operators with Site Reliability Engineering (SRE) principles.

After describing Operators and their concepts in the first chapter, we'll suggest ways to get access to a Kubernetes cluster where you can do the exercises in the rest of the book. With a cluster running, you'll deploy an Operator and observe its behavior when its application fails, scales, or gets upgraded to a new version.

Later, we will explore the Operator SDK and show you how to use it to build an Operator to naturalize an example application as a first-class Kubernetes citizen. With that practical foundation in place, we will discuss the SRE ideas from which Operators derive and the goals they share: reducing operations effort and cost, increasing service reliability, and spurring innovation by freeing teams from repetitive maintenance work.

Operator Framework and SDK

The Operator pattern emerged at CoreOS (*https://coreos.com*) as a way to automate increasingly complex applications on Kubernetes clusters, including managing Kubernetes itself and the etcd (*https://github.com/coreos/etcd*) key-value store at its heart. Work on Operators continued through an acquisition by Red Hat, leading to the 2018 release of the open source Operator Framework and SDK. The examples in this book use the Red Hat Operator SDK and the distribution mechanisms that join it in the Operator Framework.

Other Operator Tools

A community has grown up around Operators, with more than a hundred Operators for an array of applications from many vendors and projects available in Red Hat's distribution channels alone. Several other Operator construction tools exist. We won't discuss them in detail, but after you read this book you'll be able to compare any of them with the Operator SDK and Framework. Other open source tools available for building Operators include Kopf (*https://oreil.ly/JCL-S*) for Python, Kubebuilder (*https://oreil.ly/8zdbj*) from the Kubernetes project, and the Java Operator SDK (*https://oreil.ly/yXhVg*).

Conventions Used in This Book

The following typographical conventions are used in this book:

Italic
> Indicates new terms, URLs, email addresses, filenames, and file extensions.

`Constant width`
> Used for program listings, as well as within paragraphs to refer to program elements such as variable or function names, databases, data types, environment variables, statements, and keywords.

`Constant width bold`
> Shows commands or other text that should be typed literally by the user.

Constant width italic

> Shows text that should be replaced with user-supplied values or by values determined by context.

 This element signifies a tip or suggestion.

 This element signifies a general note.

 This element indicates a warning or caution.

Using Code Examples

Supplemental material (code examples, exercises, etc.) is available for download at *https://github.com/kubernetes-operators-book/*.

If you have a technical question or a problem using the code examples, please send email to *bookquestions@oreilly.com*.

This book is here to help you get your job done. In general, if example code is offered with this book, you may use it in your programs and documentation. You do not need to contact us for permission unless you're reproducing a significant portion of the code. For example, writing a program that uses several chunks of code from this book does not require permission. Selling or distributing examples from O'Reilly books does require permission. Answering a question by citing this book and quoting example code does not require permission. Incorporating a significant amount of example code from this book into your product's documentation does require permission.

We appreciate, but generally do not require, attribution. An attribution usually includes the title, author, publisher, and ISBN. For example: "*Kubernetes Operators* by Jason Dobies and Joshua Wood (O'Reilly). Copyright 2020 Red Hat, Inc., 978-1-492-04804-6."

If you feel your use of code examples falls outside fair use or the permission given above, feel free to contact us at *permissions@oreilly.com*.

O'Reilly Online Learning

O'REILLY® For more than 40 years, O'Reilly Media has provided technology and business training, knowledge, and insight to help companies succeed.

Our unique network of experts and innovators share their knowledge and expertise through books, articles, conferences, and our online learning platform. O'Reilly's online learning platform gives you on-demand access to live training courses, in-depth learning paths, interactive coding environments, and a vast collection of text and video from O'Reilly and 200+ other publishers. For more information, please visit *http://oreilly.com*.

How to Contact Us

Please address comments and questions concerning this book to the publisher:

O'Reilly Media, Inc.
1005 Gravenstein Highway North
Sebastopol, CA 95472
800-998-9938 (in the United States or Canada)
707-829-0515 (international or local)
707-829-0104 (fax)

We have a web page for this book, where we list errata, examples, and any additional information. You can access this page at *https://oreil.ly/Kubernetes_Operators*.

Email *bookquestions@oreilly.com* to comment or ask technical questions.

For more about our books, courses, and conferences, see *http://www.oreilly.com*.

Find us on Facebook: *http://facebook.com/oreilly*

Follow us on Twitter: *http://twitter.com/oreillymedia*

Watch us on YouTube: *http://www.youtube.com/oreillymedia*

Acknowledgments

We'd like to thank Red Hat and the OpenShift Advocacy team there for their support, in particular the steadfast and all-trades assistance of Ryan Jarvinen. We also thank the many people who reviewed, checked, suggested, and otherwise gave their time to make this work more coherent and complete, among them Anish Asthana, Evan Cordell, Michael Gasch, Michael Hausenblas, Shawn Hurley, and Jess Males.

CHAPTER 1

Operators Teach Kubernetes New Tricks

An Operator is a way to package, run, and maintain a Kubernetes application. A Kubernetes application is not only deployed on Kubernetes, it is designed to use and to operate in concert with Kubernetes facilities and tools.

An Operator builds on Kubernetes abstractions to automate the entire lifecycle of the software it manages. Because they extend Kubernetes, Operators provide application-specific automation in terms familiar to a large and growing community. For application programmers, Operators make it easier to deploy and run the foundation services on which their apps depend. For infrastructure engineers and vendors, Operators provide a consistent way to distribute software on Kubernetes clusters and reduce support burdens by identifying and correcting application problems before the pager beeps.

Before we begin to describe how Operators do these jobs, let's define a few Kubernetes terms to provide context and a shared language to describe Operator concepts and components.

How Kubernetes Works

Kubernetes automates the lifecycle of a stateless application, such as a static web server. Without state, any instances of an application are interchangeable. This simple web server retrieves files and sends them on to a visitor's browser. Because the server is not tracking state or storing input or data of any kind, when one server instance fails, Kubernetes can replace it with another. Kubernetes refers to these instances, each a copy of an application running on the cluster, as *replicas*.

A Kubernetes cluster is a collection of computers, called *nodes*. All cluster work runs on one, some, or all of a cluster's nodes. The basic unit of work, and of replication, is the *pod*. A pod is a group of one or more Linux containers with common resources like networking, storage, and access to shared memory.

 The Kubernetes pod documentation (*https://oreil.ly/ziz5q*) is a good starting point for more information about the pod abstraction.

At a high level, a Kubernetes cluster can be divided into two planes. The *control plane* is, in simple terms, Kubernetes itself. A collection of pods comprises the control plane and implements the Kubernetes application programming interface (API) and cluster orchestration logic.

The *application plane*, or *data plane*, is everything else. It is the group of nodes where application pods run. One or more nodes are usually dedicated to running applications, while one or more nodes are often sequestered to run only control plane pods. As with application pods, multiple replicas of control plane components can run on multiple controller nodes to provide redundancy.

The *controllers* of the control plane implement control loops that repeatedly compare the desired state of the cluster to its actual state. When the two diverge, a controller takes action to make them match. Operators extend this behavior. The schematic in Figure 1-1 shows the major control plane components, with worker nodes running application workloads.

While a strict division between the control and application planes is a convenient mental model and a common way to deploy a Kubernetes cluster to segregate workloads, the control plane components are a collection of pods running on nodes, like any other application. In small clusters, control plane components are often sharing the same node or two with application workloads.

The conceptual model of a cordoned control plane isn't quite so tidy, either. The kubelet agent running on every node is part of the control plane, for example. Likewise, an Operator is a type of controller, usually thought of as a control plane component. Operators can blur this distinct border between planes, however. Treating the control and application planes as isolated domains is a helpful simplifying abstraction, not an absolute truth.

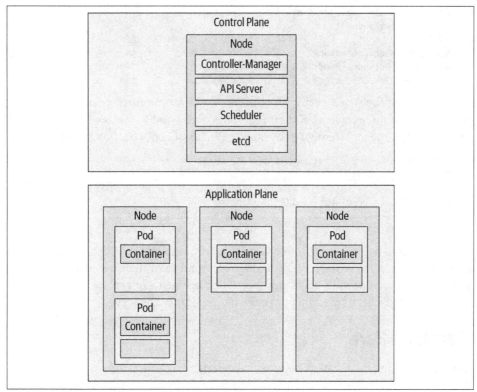

Figure 1-1. Kubernetes control plane and worker nodes

Example: Stateless Web Server

Since you haven't set up a cluster yet, the examples in this chapter are more like ter-minal excerpt "screenshots" that show what basic interactions between Kubernetes and an application look like. You are not expected to execute these commands as you are those throughout the rest of the book. In this first example, Kubernetes manages a relatively simple application and no Operators are involved.

Consider a cluster running a single replica of a stateless, static web server:

```
$ kubectl get pods>
NAME                        READY    STATUS    RESTARTS    AGE

staticweb-69ccd6d6c-9mr8l   1/1      Running   0           23s
```

After declaring there should be three replicas, the cluster's actual state differs from the desired state, and Kubernetes starts two new instances of the web server to recon-cile the two, scaling the web server deployment:

```
$ kubectl scale deployment staticweb --replicas=3
$ kubectl get pods
NAME                        READY   STATUS    RESTARTS   AGE
staticweb-69ccd6d6c-4tdhk   1/1     Running   0          6s
staticweb-69ccd6d6c-9mr8l   1/1     Running   0          100s
staticweb-69ccd6d6c-m9qc7   1/1     Running   0          6s
```

Deleting one of the web server pods triggers work in the control plane to restore the desired state of three replicas. Kubernetes starts a new pod to replace the deleted one. In this excerpt, the replacement pod shows a STATUS of ContainerCreating:

```
$ kubectl delete pod staticweb-69ccd6d6c-9mr8l
$ kubectl get pods
NAME                        READY   STATUS             RESTARTS   AGE
staticweb-69ccd6d6c-4tdhk   1/1     Running            0          2m8s
staticweb-69ccd6d6c-bk27p   0/1     ContainerCreating  0          14s
staticweb-69ccd6d6c-m9qc7   1/1     Running            0          2m8s
```

This static site's web server is interchangeable with any other replica, or with a new pod that replaces one of the replicas. It doesn't store data or maintain state in any way. Kubernetes doesn't need to make any special arrangements to replace a failed pod, or to scale the application by adding or removing replicas of the server.

Stateful Is Hard

Most applications have state. They also have particulars of startup, component inter-dependence, and configuration. They often have their own notion of what "cluster" means. They need to reliably store critical and sometimes voluminous data. Those are just three of the dimensions in which real-world applications must maintain state. It would be ideal to manage these applications with uniform mechanisms while auto-mating their complex storage, networking, and cluster connection requirements.

Kubernetes cannot know all about every stateful, complex, clustered application while also remaining general, adaptable, and simple. It aims instead to provide a set of flexi-ble abstractions, covering the basic application concepts of scheduling, replication, and failover automation, while providing a clean extension mechanism for more advanced or application-specific operations. Kubernetes, on its own, does not and should not know the configuration values for, say, a PostgreSQL database cluster, with its arranged memberships and stateful, persistent storage.

Operators Are Software SREs

Site Reliability Engineering (SRE) is a set of patterns and principles for running large systems. Originating at Google, SRE has had a pronounced influence on industry practice. Practitioners must interpret and apply SRE philosophy to particular circum-stances, but a key tenet is automating systems administration by writing software to run your software. Teams freed from rote maintenance work have more time to create new features, fix bugs, and generally improve their products.

An Operator is like an automated Site Reliability Engineer for its application. It encodes in software the skills of an expert administrator. An Operator can manage a cluster of database servers, for example. It knows the details of configuring and managing its application, and it can install a database cluster of a declared software version and number of members. An Operator continues to monitor its application as it runs, and can back up data, recover from failures, and upgrade the application over time, automatically. Cluster users employ kubectl and other standard tools to work with Operators and the applications they manage, because Operators extend Kubernetes.

How Operators Work

Operators work by extending the Kubernetes control plane and API. In its simplest form, an Operator adds an endpoint to the Kubernetes API, called a *custom resource* (CR), along with a control plane component that monitors and maintains resources of the new type. This Operator can then take action based on the resource's state. This is illustrated in Figure 1-2.

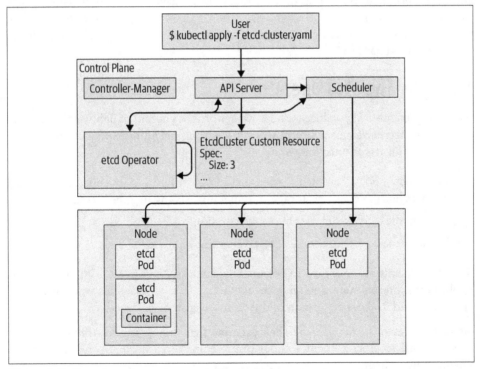

Figure 1-2. Operators are custom controllers watching a custom resource

Kubernetes CRs

CRs are the API extension mechanism in Kubernetes. A *custom resource definition* (CRD) defines a CR; it's analogous to a schema for the CR data. Unlike members of the official API, a given CRD doesn't exist on every Kubernetes cluster. CRDs extend the API of the particular cluster where they are defined. CRs provide endpoints for reading and writing structured data. A cluster user can interact with CRs with `kubectl` or another Kubernetes client, just like any other API resource.

How Operators Are Made

Kubernetes compares a set of resources to reality; that is, the running state of the cluster. It takes actions to make reality match the desired state described by those resources. Operators extend that pattern to specific applications on specific clusters. An Operator is a custom Kubernetes controller watching a CR type and taking application-specific actions to make reality match the `spec` in that resource.

Making an Operator means creating a CRD and providing a program that runs in a loop watching CRs of that kind. What the Operator does in response to changes in the CR is specific to the application the Operator manages. The actions an Operator performs can include almost anything: scaling a complex app, application version upgrades, or even managing kernel modules for nodes in a computational cluster with specialized hardware.

Example: The etcd Operator

etcd is a distributed key-value store. In other words, it's a kind of lightweight database cluster. An etcd cluster usually requires a knowledgeable administrator to manage it. An etcd administrator must know how to:

- Join a new node to an etcd cluster, including configuring its endpoints, making connections to persistent storage, and making existing members aware of it.
- Back up the etcd cluster data and configuration.
- Upgrade the etcd cluster to new etcd versions.

The etcd Operator knows how to perform those tasks. An Operator knows about its application's internal state, and takes regular action to align that state with the desired state expressed in the specification of one or more custom resources.

As in the previous example, the shell excerpts that follow are illustrative, and you won't be able to execute them without prior setup. You'll do that setup and run an Operator in Chapter 2.

The Case of the Missing Member

Since the etcd Operator understands etcd's state, it can recover from an etcd cluster member's failure in the same way Kubernetes replaced the deleted stateless web server pod in our earlier example. Assume there is a three-member etcd cluster managed by the etcd Operator. The Operator itself and the etcd cluster members run as pods:

```
$ kubectl get pods
NAME                                   READY   STATUS    RESTARTS   AGE
etcd-operator-6f44498865-lv7b9         1/1     Running   0          1h
example-etcd-cluster-cpnwr62qgl        1/1     Running   0          1h
example-etcd-cluster-fff78tmpxr        1/1     Running   0          1h
example-etcd-cluster-lrlk7xwb2k        1/1     Running   0          1h
```

Deleting an etcd pod triggers a reconciliation, and the etcd Operator knows how to recover to the desired state of three replicas—something Kubernetes can't do alone. But unlike with the blank-slate restart of a stateless web server, the Operator has to arrange the new etcd pod's cluster membership, configuring it for the existing endpoints and establishing it with the remaining etcd members:

```
$ kubectl delete pod example-etcd-cluster-cpnwr62qgl
$ kubectl get pods
NAME                                   READY   STATUS           RESTARTS   AGE
etcd-operator-6f44498865-lv7b9         1/1     Running          0          1h
example-etcd-cluster-fff78tmpxr        1/1     Running          0          1h
example-etcd-cluster-lrlk7xwb2k        1/1     Running          0          1h
example-etcd-cluster-r6cb8g2qqw        0/1     PodInitializing  0          4s    ❶
```

❶ The replacement pod is in the PodInitializing state.

The etcd API remains available to clients as the Operator repairs the etcd cluster. In Chapter 2, you'll deploy the etcd Operator and put it through its paces while using the etcd API to read and write data. For now, it's worth remembering that adding a member to a running etcd cluster isn't as simple as just running a new etcd pod, and the etcd Operator hides that complexity and automatically heals the etcd cluster.

Who Are Operators For?

The Operator pattern arose in response to infrastructure engineers and developers wanting to extend Kubernetes to provide features specific to their sites and software. Operators make it easier for cluster administrators to enable, and developers to use, foundation software pieces like databases and storage systems with less management overhead. If the "killernewdb" database server that's perfect for your application's backend has an Operator to manage it, you can deploy killernewdb without needing to become an expert killernewdb DBA.

Application developers build Operators to manage the applications they are delivering, simplifying the deployment and management experience on their customers'

Kubernetes clusters. Infrastructure engineers create Operators to control deployed services and systems.

Operator Adoption

A wide variety of developers and companies have adopted the Operator pattern, and there are already many Operators available that make it easier to use key services as components of your applications. CrunchyData has developed an Operator that manages PostgreSQL database clusters. There are popular Operators for MongoDB and Redis. Rook manages Ceph storage on Kubernetes clusters, while other Operators provide on-cluster management of external storage services like Amazon S3.

Moreover, Kubernetes-based distributions like Red Hat's OpenShift use Operators to build features atop a Kubernetes core, keeping the OpenShift web console available and up to date, for example. On the user side, OpenShift has added mechanisms for point-and-click Operator installation and use in the web console, and for Operator developers to hook into the OperatorHub.io (*https://operatorhub.io*), discussed in Chapter 8 and Chapter 10.

Let's Get Going!

Operators need a Kubernetes cluster to run on. In the next chapter we'll show you a few different ways to get access to a cluster, whether it's a local virtual Kubernetes on your laptop, a complete installation on some number of nodes, or an external service. Once you have admin access to a Kubernetes cluster, you will deploy the etcd Operator and see how it manages an etcd cluster on your behalf.

CHAPTER 2

Running Operators

In the first section of this chapter we outline the requirements for running the examples in this book, and offer advice on how to establish access to a Kubernetes cluster that satisfies those requirements. In the second section, you'll use that cluster to investigate what Operators do by installing and using one.

By the end, you'll have a Kubernetes cluster to use as an Operator test bed, and you'll know how to deploy an existing Operator on it from a set of manifests. You'll also have seen an Operator managing its application's specific internal state in the face of changes and failures, informing your understanding of the Operator architecture and build tools presented in succeeding chapters.

Setting Up an Operator Lab

To build, test, and run Operators in the following chapters, you'll need `cluster-admin` access to a cluster running Kubernetes version v1.11.0 or later. If you've already met these requirements, you can skip ahead to the next section. In this section we offer general advice to readers who need to set up a Kubernetes cluster, or who need a local environment for Operator development and testing.

Cluster Version Requirements

We've tested the examples in this book with Kubernetes releases v1.11 up to v1.16. We will state when any feature or action we examine requires a release later than v1.11.

Control plane extensibility

Kubernetes version 1.2 introduced the API extension mechanism known as the CRD in elemental form as the *third party resource* (TPR). Since then, the components Operators build on have multiplied and matured, as illustrated in Figure 2-1. CRDs were formalized with the Kubernetes version 1.7 release.

Extensibility Feature x Kubernetes Release	v1.2	v1.3	v1.4	v1.5	v1.6	v1.7	v1.8	v1.9	v1.10	v1.11	v1.12	v1.13	v1.14	v1.15	v1.16
CRD resource validation													Beta		
CRD schema conversion webhook													Alpha	Beta	
CRD server-side print columns										Alpha	Stable				
CRD API versioning										Alpha	Stable				
Custom Resource Definitions						Alpha	Beta								Stable
Third Party Resources	Alpha	Beta					Deprecated								

Figure 2-1. Extensibility features per Kubernetes release

As you saw in Chapter 1, a CRD is the definition of a new, site-specific resource (or API endpoint) in the Kubernetes API of a particular cluster. CRDs are one of two essential building blocks for the most basic description of the Operator pattern: a custom controller managing CRs.

Authorization Requirements

Since Operators extend Kubernetes itself, you'll need privileged, cluster-wide access to a Kubernetes cluster to deploy them, such as the common `cluster-admin` cluster role.

 Less privileged users can use the services and applications that Operators manage—the "operands."

While you should configure more granular Kubernetes Role-Based Access Control (RBAC) for production scenarios, having complete control of your cluster means you'll be able to deploy CRDs and Operators immediately. You'll also have the power to declare more detailed RBAC as you develop the roles, service accounts, and bindings for your Operators and the applications they manage.

You can ask the Kubernetes API about the `cluster-admin` role to see if it exists on your cluster. The following shell excerpt shows how to get a summary of the role with the kubectl's `describe` subcommand:

```
$ kubectl describe clusterrole cluster-admin
Name:          cluster-admin  ❶
Labels:        kubernetes.io/bootstrapping=rbac-defaults
PolicyRule:
  Resources  Non-Resource URLs  Resource Names  Verbs
  ---------  -----------------  --------------  -----
  *.*        []                 []              [*]
             [*]                []              [*]
```

❶ The RBAC cluster-admin ClusterRole: anything goes.

Standard Tools and Techniques

Operators aim to make the complex applications they manage first-class citizens of the Kubernetes API. We show what that means in the following chapters' examples. At this stage, it means that a recent version of the command-line Kubernetes API tool, kubectl, is the only requirement for deploying and interacting with basic Operators on your cluster.

Readers who need to install or update kubectl should consult the current kubectl documentation (*https://oreil.ly/ke6KM*).

> Users of the Red Hat OpenShift Kubernetes distribution (described below) may optionally (and interchangeably) use the oc OpenShift API utility in place of kubectl.

Suggested Cluster Configurations

There are many ways to run a Kubernetes cluster where you can deploy Operators. As mentioned previously, if you are already running a recent Kubernetes version, you can skip past this advice and on to "Running a Simple Operator" on page 13. If you aren't, we have tested the Kubernetes packagings or distributions described in this section enough to expect they will support the exercises in this book.

Minikube

Minikube v1.5.2 (*https://oreil.ly/dBPzK*) deploys Kubernetes v1.16.2. It runs a single-node Kubernetes cluster in a virtual machine (VM) on your local system's hypervisor. By default, Minikube expects to use VirtualBox because of its wide availability, but with a few extra steps it can also use your platform's native hypervisor, like KVM on Linux, Hyper-V on Windows, or HyperKit and Hypervisor.framework on macOS. We avoid detailed installation instructions here, because they are better left to the Minikube documentation (*https://oreil.ly/eRZpQ*). We have tested the examples in this book most thoroughly with Minikube, and for reasons of convenience and cost we are recommending that you start your Operator experiments with a local environment like it, CodeReady Containers (see the next section), or with Kubernetes in Docker (kind) (*https://oreil.ly/2y6PD*).

Red Hat OpenShift

OpenShift is Red Hat's distribution of Kubernetes. Anything you can do on Kubernetes, you can do on OpenShift of an equivalent core version. (There are also OpenShift-specific features built atop Kubernetes, but those are beyond the scope of this book.) OpenShift version 4 provides a full-featured Kubernetes distribution that is itself designed, delivered, and managed using Operators. It's a "self-hosted" Kubernetes, capable of performing in-place platform upgrades without incurring downtime for hosted workloads. OpenShift includes Operator Lifecycle Manager, described in Chapter 4, and a graphical interface to the Operator Catalog distribution mechanism out of the box.

You can deploy a fully fledged OpenShift v4 cluster on Amazon Web Services (AWS), Microsoft Azure, or Google Cloud Platform with a free trial license by visiting Red Hat's *https://try.openshift.com*.

> To run OpenShift on your laptop, take a look at Minikube's equivalent, Red Hat CodeReady Containers (*https://github.com/codeready/crc*).

OpenShift Learning Portal

The OpenShift learning portal offers guided lessons, including access to a cluster with all the necessary privileges for installing, deploying, and managing Operators. Scenarios are available in your web browser, making it easy to keep learning beyond the examples in this book. An OpenShift cluster spins up for each session, and you're given command-line and web GUI access to it.

To check it out, visit *https://learn.openshift.com* and select the "Building Operators on OpenShift" group of topics.

Checking Your Cluster Version

Verify that your cluster is running Kubernetes version v1.11 or later by running `kubectl version`. This command will return one API version string for your `kubectl` binary and a second version string for the cluster to which it is connecting:

```
$ kubectl version
Client Version: version.Info{Major:"1", Minor:"16", GitVersion:"v1.16.2",
GitCommit:"c97fe5036ef3df2967d086711e6c0c405941e14b", GitTreeState:"clean",
BuildDate:"2019-10-15T19:18:23Z", GoVersion:"go1.12.10", Compiler:"gc",
Platform:"darwin/amd64"}
Server Version: version.Info{Major:"1", Minor:"16", GitVersion:"v1.16.2",
GitCommit:"c97fe5036ef3df2967d086711e6c0c405941e14b", GitTreeState:"clean",
BuildDate:"2019-10-15T19:09:08Z", GoVersion:"go1.12.10", Compiler:"gc",
Platform:"linux/amd64"}
```

In the preceding output, both client and server are running Kubernetes version
1.16.2. While a kubectl client up to one release behind the server should work
(*https://oreil.ly/I7K1e*), for simplicity, you should make sure your client and server
minor versions match. If you have v1.11 or later, you're ready to start experimenting
with Operators.

Running a Simple Operator

Once you've verified that you have privileged access to a Kubernetes cluster of a compatible version, you're ready to deploy an Operator and see what Operators can do.
You'll see the skeleton of this same procedure again later, when you deploy and test
the Operator you build. The etcd Operator's straightforward automation of recovery
and upgrades shows the principles and goals of Kubernetes Operators in action.

A Common Starting Point

etcd (*https://github.com/coreos/etcd*) is a distributed key-value store with roots at
CoreOS, now under the auspices of the Cloud Native Computing Foundation. It is
the underlying data store at the core of Kubernetes, and a key piece of several distributed applications. etcd provides reliable storage by implementing a protocol
called Raft (*https://raft.github.io/*) that guarantees consensus among a quorum of
members.

The etcd Operator often serves as a kind of "Hello World" example of the value and
mechanics of the Operator pattern, and we follow that tradition here. We return to it
because the most basic use of etcd is not difficult to illustrate, but etcd cluster setup
and administration require exactly the kind of application-specific know-how you
can bake into an Operator. To use etcd, you *put* keys and values in, and *get* them back
out by name. Creating a reliable etcd cluster of the minimum three or more nodes
requires configuration of endpoints, auth, and other concerns usually left to an etcd
expert (or their collection of custom shell scripts). Keeping etcd running and upgraded over time requires continued administration. The etcd Operator knows how to
do all of this.

In the sections that follow, you'll deploy the etcd Operator, then have it create an etcd
cluster according to your specifications. You will have the Operator recover from

failures and perform a version upgrade while the etcd API continues to service read and write requests, showing how an Operator automates the lifecycle of a piece of foundation software.

 You can follow this example on a running OpenShift cluster without doing any setup at the OpenShift learning portal (*https://oreil.ly/j-xKh*).

Fetching the etcd Operator Manifests

This book provides an accompanying Git repository (*https://github.com/kubernetes-operators-book/chapters.git*) for each chapter's example code. Grab the *chapters* repo and change into Chapter 3's examples directory, as shown here:

```
$ git clone https://github.com/kubernetes-operators-book/chapters.git
$ cd chapters/ch03
```

CRs: Custom API Endpoints

As with nearly everything in Kubernetes, a YAML manifest describes a CRD. A CR is a named endpoint in the Kubernetes API. A CRD named etcdclusters.etcd.data base.coreos.com represents the new type of endpoint.

Creating a CRD

A CRD defines the types and values within an instance of a CR. This example defines a new *kind* of resource, the EtcdCluster.

Use cat, less, or your preferred pager to read the file named *etcd-operator-crd.yaml*. You'll see something like the following, the YAML that specifies the EtcdCluster CRD:

```
apiVersion: apiextensions.k8s.io/v1beta1
kind: CustomResourceDefinition
metadata:
  name: etcdclusters.etcd.database.coreos.com
spec:
  group: etcd.database.coreos.com
  names:
    kind: EtcdCluster
    listKind: EtcdClusterList
    plural: etcdclusters
    shortNames:
    - etcdclus
    - etcd
    singular: etcdcluster
  scope: Namespaced
  versions:
```

```
  - name: v1beta2
    served: true
    storage: true
```

The CRD defines how the Kubernetes API should reference this new resource. The shortened nicknames that help you do a little less typing in kubectl are defined here, too.

Create the CRD on your cluster:

```
$ kubectl create -f etcd-operator-crd.yaml
```

A quick check shows the new CRD, etcdclusters.etcd.database.coreos.com:

```
$ kubectl get crd
NAME                                      CREATED AT
etcdclusters.etcd.database.coreos.com     2019-11-15T02:50:14Z
```

 The CR's group, version, and kind together form the fully qualified name of a Kubernetes resource type. That canonical name must be unique across a cluster. The CRD you created represents a resource in the etcd.database.coreos.com group, of version v1beta2 and kind EtcdCluster.

Who Am I: Defining an Operator Service Account

In Chapter 3 we give an overview of Kubernetes authorization and define service accounts, roles, and other authorization concepts. For now, we just want to take a first look at basic declarations for a service account and the capabilities that account needs to run the etcd Operator.

The file *etcd-operator-sa.yaml* defines the service account:

```
apiVersion: v1
kind: ServiceAccount
metadata:
  name: etcd-operator-sa
```

Create the service account by using kubectl create:

```
$ kubectl create -f etcd-operator-sa.yaml
serviceaccount/etcd-operator-sa created
```

If you check the list of cluster service accounts, you'll see that it appears:

```
$ kubectl get serviceaccounts
NAME               SECRETS   AGE
builder            2         2h
default            3         2h
deployer           2         2h
etcd-operator-sa   2         3s
[...]
```

The role

The role governing the service account is defined in a file named *etcd-operator-role.yaml*. We'll leave aside a detailed discussion of RBAC for later chapters and Appendix C, but the key items are fairly visible in the role manifest. We give the role a name that we'll use to reference it from other places: etcd-operator-role. The YAML goes on to list the kinds of resources the role may use, and what it can do with them, that is, what verbs it can say:

```
apiVersion: rbac.authorization.k8s.io/v1
kind: Role
metadata:
  name: etcd-operator-role
rules:
- apiGroups:
  - etcd.database.coreos.com
  resources:
  - etcdclusters
  - etcdbackups
  - etcdrestores
  verbs:
  - '*'
- apiGroups:
  - ""
  resources:
  - pods
  - services
  - endpoints
  - persistentvolumeclaims
  - events
  verbs:
  - '*'
- apiGroups:
  - apps
  resources:
  - deployments
  verbs:
  - '*'
- apiGroups:
  - ""
  resources:
  - secrets
  verbs:
  - get
```

As with the service account, create the role with kubectl:

```
$ kubectl create -f etcd-operator-role.yaml
role.rbac.authorization.k8s.io/etcd-operator-role created
```

Role binding

The last bit of RBAC configuration, RoleBinding, assigns the role to the service account for the etcd Operator. It's declared in the file *etcd-operator-rolebinding.yaml*:

```
apiVersion: rbac.authorization.k8s.io/v1
kind: RoleBinding
metadata:
  name: etcd-operator-rolebinding
roleRef:
  apiGroup: rbac.authorization.k8s.io
  kind: Role
  name: etcd-operator-role
subjects:
- kind: ServiceAccount
  name: etcd-operator-sa
  namespace: default
```

Notice the last line. If you're on a brand-new OpenShift cluster, like that provided by CodeReady Containers, by default your `kubectl` or `oc` commands will run in the namespace `myproject`. If you're on a similarly unconfigured Kubernetes cluster, your context's default will usually be the namespace `default`. Wherever you are, the `namespace` value in this RoleBinding must match the namespace on the cluster where you are working.

Create the binding now:

```
$ kubectl create -f etcd-operator-rolebinding.yaml
rolebinding.rbac.authorization.k8s.io/etcd-operator-rolebinding created
```

Deploying the etcd Operator

The Operator is a custom controller running in a pod, and it watches the EtcdCluster CR you defined earlier. The manifest file *etcd-operator-deployment.yaml* lays out the Operator pod's specification, including the container image for the Operator you're deploying. Notice that it does not define the spec for the etcd cluster. You'll describe the desired etcd cluster to the deployed etcd Operator in a CR once the Operator is running:

```
apiVersion: extensions/v1beta1
kind: Deployment
metadata:
  labels:
    name: etcdoperator
  name: etcd-operator
spec:
  replicas: 1
  selector:
      name: etcd-operator
  template:
        name: etcd-operator
```

```
spec:
  containers:
  - name: etcd-operator
    image: quay.io/coreos/etcd-operator:v0.9.4
    command:
    - etcd-operator
    - --create-crd=false
    [...]
    imagePullPolicy: IfNotPresent
    serviceAccountName: etcd-operator-sa
```

The deployment provides labels and a name for your Operator. Some key items to note here are the container image to run in this deployment's pods, etcd-operator:v0.9.4, and the service account the deployment's resources should use to access the cluster's Kubernetes API. The etcd-operator deployment uses the etcd-operator-sa service account created for it.

As usual, you can create this resource on the cluster from the manifest:

```
$ kubectl create -f etcd-operator-deployment.yaml
deployment.apps/etcd-operator created
$ kubectl get deployments
NAME            DESIRED    CURRENT    UP-TO-DATE    AVAILABLE    AGE
etcd-operator   1          1          1             1            19s
```

The etcd Operator is itself a pod running in that deployment. Here you can see it starting up:

```
$ kubectl get pods
NAME                              READY    STATUS              RESTARTS    AGE
etcd-operator-594fbd565f-4fm8k    0/1      ContainerCreating   0           4s
```

Declaring an etcd Cluster

Earlier, you created a CRD defining a new kind of resource, an EtcdCluster. Now that you have an Operator watching EtcdCluster resources, you can declare an EtcdCluster with your desired state. To do so, provide the two spec elements the Operator recognizes: size, the number of etcd cluster members, and the version of etcd each of those members should run.

You can see the spec stanza in the file *etcd-cluster-cr.yaml*:

```
apiVersion: etcd.database.coreos.com/v1beta2
kind: EtcdCluster
metadata:
  name: example-etcd-cluster
spec:
  size: 3
  version: 3.1.10
```

This brief manifest declares a desired state of three cluster members, each running version 3.1.10 of the etcd server. Create this etcd cluster using the familiar kubectl syntax:

```
$ kubectl create -f etcd-cluster-cr.yaml
etcdcluster.etcd.database.coreos.com/example-etcd-cluster created
$ kubectl get pods -w
NAME                                READY  STATUS   RESTARTS  AGE
etcd-operator-594fbd565f-4fm8k      1/1    Running  0         3m
example-etcd-cluster-95gqrthjbz     1/1    Running  2         38s
example-etcd-cluster-m9ftnsk572     1/1    Running  0         34s
example-etcd-cluster-pjqhm8d4qj     1/1    Running  0         31s
```

This example etcd cluster is a first-class citizen, an `EtcdCluster` in your cluster's API. Since it's an API resource, you can get the etcd cluster spec and status directly from Kubernetes. Try kubectl `describe` to report on the size, etcd version, and status of your etcd cluster, as shown here:

```
$ kubectl describe etcdcluster/example-etcd-cluster
Name:         example-etcd-cluster
Namespace:    default
API Version:  etcd.database.coreos.com/v1beta2
Kind:         EtcdCluster
[...]
Spec:
  Repository:  quay.io/coreos/etcd
  Size:        3
  Version:     3.1.10
Status:
  Client Port:  2379
  Conditions:
    Last Transition Time:  2019-11-15T02:52:04Z
    Reason:                Cluster available
    Status:                True
    Type:                  Available
  Current Version:  3.1.10
  Members:
    Ready:
      example-etcd-cluster-6pq7qn82g2
      example-etcd-cluster-dbwt7kr8lw
      example-etcd-cluster-t85hs2hwzb
  Phase:         Running
  Service Name:  example-etcd-cluster-client
```

Exercising etcd

You now have a running etcd cluster. The etcd Operator creates a Kubernetes *service* (*https://oreil.ly/meXW_*) in the etcd cluster's namespace. A service is an endpoint where clients can obtain access to a group of pods, even though the members of the group may change. A service by default has a DNS name visible in the cluster. The

Operator constructs the name of the service used by clients of the etcd API by appending `-client` to the etcd cluster name defined in the CR. Here, the client service is named `example-etcd-cluster-client`, and it listens on the usual etcd client IP port, 2379. Kubectl can list the services associated with the etcd cluster:

```
$ kubectl get services --selector etcd_cluster=example-etcd-cluster
NAME                          TYPE        CLUSTER-IP    ... PORT(S)            AGE
example-etcd-cluster          ClusterIP   None          ... 2379/TCP,2380/TCP  21h
example-etcd-cluster-client   ClusterIP   10.96.46.231  ... 2379/TCP           21h
```

> The other service created by the etcd Operator, `example-etcd-cluster`, is utilized by etcd cluster members rather than etcd API clients.

You can run the etcd client on the cluster and use it to connect to the client service and interact with the etcd API. The following command lands you in the shell of an etcd container:

```
$ kubectl run --rm -i --tty etcdctl --image quay.io/coreos/etcd \
    --restart=Never -- /bin/sh
```

From the etcd container's shell, create and read a key-value pair in etcd with etcdctl's put and get verbs:

```
$ export ETCDCTL_API=3
$ export ETCDCSVC=http://example-etcd-cluster-client:2379
$ etcdctl --endpoints $ETCDCSVC put foo bar
$ etcdctl --endpoints $ETCDCSVC get foo
foo
bar
```

Repeat these queries or run new put and get commands in an `etcdctl` shell after each of the changes you go on to make. You'll see the continuing availability of the etcd API service as the etcd Operator grows the cluster, replaces members, and upgrades the version of etcd.

Scaling the etcd Cluster

You can grow the etcd cluster by changing the declared `size` specification. Edit *etcd-cluster-cr.yaml* and change `size` from 3 to 4 etcd members. Apply the changes to the EtcdCluster CR:

```
$ kubectl apply -f etcd-cluster-cr.yaml
```

Checking the running pods shows the Operator adding a new etcd member to the etcd cluster:

```
$ kubectl get pods
NAME                                READY  STATUS    RESTARTS  AGE
etcd-operator-594fbd565f-4fm8k      1/1    Running   1         16m
example-etcd-cluster-95gqrthjbz     1/1    Running   2         15m
example-etcd-cluster-m9ftnsk572     1/1    Running   0         15m
example-etcd-cluster-pjqhm8d4qj     1/1    Running   0         15m
example-etcd-cluster-w5l67llqq8     0/1    Init:0/1  0         3s
```

 You can also try kubectl edit etcdcluster/example-etcd-cluster to drop into an editor and make a live change to the cluster size.

Failure and Automated Recovery

You saw the etcd Operator replace a failed member back in Chapter 1. Before you see it live, it's worth reiterating the general steps you'd have to take to handle this manually. Unlike a stateless program, no etcd pod runs in a vacuum. Usually, a human etcd "operator" has to notice a member's failure, execute a new copy, and provide it with configuration so it can join the etcd cluster with the remaining members. The etcd Operator understands etcd's internal state and makes the recovery automatic.

Recovering from a failed etcd member

Run a quick kubectl get pods -l app=etc to get a list of the pods in your etcd cluster. Pick one you don't like the looks of, and tell Kubernetes to delete it:

```
$ kubectl delete pod example-etcd-cluster-95gqrthjbz
pod "example-etcd-cluster-95gqrthjbz" deleted
```

The Operator notices the difference between reality on the cluster and the desired state, and adds an etcd member to replace the one you deleted. You can see the new etcd cluster member in the PodInitializing state when retrieving the list of pods, as shown here:

```
$ kubectl get pods -w
NAME                                READY  STATUS          RESTARTS  AGE
etcd-operator-594fbd565f-4fm8k      1/1    Running         1         18m
example-etcd-cluster-m9ftnsk572     1/1    Running         0         17m
example-etcd-cluster-pjqhm8d4qj     1/1    Running         0         17m
example-etcd-cluster-r6cb8g2qqw     0/1    PodInitializing 0         31s
```

The -w switch tells kubectl to "watch" the list of pods and to print updates on its standard output with every change to the list. You can stop the watch and return to your shell prompt with Ctrl-C.

You can check the Events to see the recovery actions logged in the example-etcd-cluster CR:

```
$ kubectl describe etcdcluster/example-etcd-cluster
[...]
Events:
  Normal  Replacing Dead Member  4m    etcd-operator-589c65bd9f-hpkc6
    The dead member example-etcd-cluster-95gqrthjbz is being replaced
  Normal  Member Removed         4m    etcd-operator-589c65bd9f-hpkc6
    Existing member example-etcd-cluster-95gqrthjbz removed from the cluster
[...]
```

Throughout the recovery process, if you fire up the etcd client pod again, you can make requests to the etcd cluster, including a check on its general health:

```
$ kubectl run --rm -i --tty etcdctl --image quay.io/coreos/etcd \
  --restart=Never -- /bin/sh
If you don't see a command prompt, try pressing enter.
$ etcdctl --endpoints http://example-etcd-cluster-client:2379 cluster-health
member 5ee0dd47065a4f55 is healthy: got healthy result ...
member 70baca4290889c4a is healthy: got healthy result ...
member 76cd6c58798a7a4b is healthy: got healthy result ...
cluster is healthy
$ exit
pod "etcdctl" deleted
```

The etcd Operator recovers from failures in its complex, stateful application the same way Kubernetes automates recoveries for stateless apps. That is conceptually simple but operationally powerful. Building on these concepts, Operators can perform more advanced tricks, like upgrading the software they manage. Automating upgrades can have a positive impact on security, just by making sure things stay up to date. When an Operator performs rolling upgrades of its application while maintaining service availability, it's easier to keep software patched with the latest fixes.

Upgrading etcd Clusters

If you happen to be an etcd user already, you may have noticed we specified an older version, 3.1.10. We contrived this so we could explore the etcd Operator's upgrade skills.

Upgrading the hard way

At this point, you have an etcd cluster running version 3.1.10. To upgrade to etcd 3.2.13, you need to perform a series of steps. Since this book is about Operators, and not etcd administration, we've condensed the process presented here, leaving aside networking and host-level concerns to outline the manual upgrade process. The steps to follow to upgrade manually are:

1. Check the version and health of each etcd node.

2. Create a snapshot of the cluster state for disaster recovery.

3. Stop one etcd server. Replace the existing version with the v3.2.13 binary. Start the new version.

4. Repeat for each etcd cluster member—at least two more times in a three-member cluster.

For the gory details, see the etcd upgrade documentation (*https://oreil.ly/II9Pn*).

The easy way: Let the Operator do it

With a sense of the repetitive and error-prone process of a manual upgrade, it's easier to see the power of encoding that etcd-specific knowledge in the etcd Operator. The Operator can manage the etcd version, and an upgrade becomes a matter of declaring a new desired version in an EtcdCluster resource.

Triggering etcd upgrades

Get the version of the current etcd container image by querying some `etcd-cluster` pod, filtering the output to see just the version:

```
$ kubectl get pod example-etcd-cluster-795649v9kq \
  -o yaml | grep "image:" | uniq
image: quay.io/coreos/etcd:v3.1.10
image: busybox:1.28.0-glibc
```

Or, since you added an EtcdCluster resource to the Kubernetes API, you can instead summarize the Operator's picture of `example-etcd-cluster` directly by using `kubectl describe` as you did earlier:

```
$ kubectl describe etcdcluster/example-etcd-cluster
```

You'll see the cluster is running etcd version 3.1.10, as specified in the file *etcd-cluster-cr.yaml* and the CR created from it.

Edit `etcd-cluster-cr.yaml` and change the `version` spec from `3.1.10` to `3.2.13`. Then apply the new spec to the resource on the cluster:

```
$ kubectl apply -f etcd-cluster-cr.yaml
```

Use the `describe` command again and take a look at the current and target versions, as well as the member upgrade notices in the `Events` stanza:

```
$ kubectl describe etcdcluster/example-etcd-cluster
Name:          example-etcd-cluster
Namespace:     default
API Version:   etcd.database.coreos.com/v1beta2
Kind:          EtcdCluster
[...]
Status:
  Conditions:
    [...]
```

```
    Message:                upgrading to 3.2.13
    Reason:                 Cluster upgrading
    Status:                 True
    Type:                   Upgrading
  Current Version:          3.1.10
  [...]
  Size:            3
  Target Version:  3.2.13
Events:
  Type    Reason            Age  From                         ...
  ----    ------            ---  ----                         ---
  Normal  Member Upgraded   3s   etcd-operator-594fbd565f-4fm8k ...
  Normal  Member Upgraded   5s   etcd-operator-594fbd565f-4fm8k ...
```

Upgrade the upgrade

With some kubectl tricks, you can make the same edit directly through the Kubernetes API. This time, let's upgrade from 3.2.13 to the latest minor version of etcd available at the time of this writing, version 3.3.12:

```
$ kubectl patch etcdcluster example-etcd-cluster --type='json' \
  -p '[{"op": "replace", "path": "/spec/version", "value":3.3.12}]'
```

Remember you can always make this change in the etcd cluster's CR manifest and then apply it with kubectl, as you did to trigger the first upgrade.

Consecutive kubectl describe etcdcluster/example-etcd-cluster commands will show the transition from the old version to a target version until that becomes the current version, at which point you'll see Current Version: 3.3.12. The Events section records each of those upgrades:

```
Normal  Member Upgraded   1m    etcd-operator-594fbd565f-4fm8k
   Member example-etcd-cluster-pjqhm8d4qj upgraded from 3.1.10 to 3.2.23
Normal  Member Upgraded   27s   etcd-operator-594fbd565f-4fm8k
   Member example-etcd-cluster-r6cb8g2qqw upgraded from 3.2.23 to 3.3.12
```

Cleaning Up

Before proceeding, it will be helpful if you remove the resources you created and manipulated to experiment with the etcd Operator. As shown in the following shell excerpt, you can remove resources with the manifests used to create them. First, ensure your current working directory is *ch03* inside the *chapters* Git repository you cloned earlier (cd chapters/ch03):

```
$ kubectl delete -f etcd-operator-sa.yaml
$ kubectl delete -f etcd-operator-role.yaml
$ kubectl delete -f etcd-operator-rolebinding.yaml
$ kubectl delete -f etcd-operator-crd.yaml
$ kubectl delete -f etcd-operator-deployment.yaml
$ kubectl delete -f etcd-cluster-cr.yaml
serviceaccount "etcd-operator-sa" deleted
```

```
role.rbac.authorization.k8s.io "etcd-operator-role" deleted
rolebinding.rbac.authorization.k8s.io "etcd-operator-rolebinding" deleted
customresourcedefinition.apiextensions.k8s.io \
  "etcdclusters.etcd.database.coreos.com" deleted
deployment.apps "etcd-operator" deleted
etcdcluster.etcd.database.coreos.com "example-etcd-cluster" deleted
```

Summary

We use the etcd API here with the `etcdctl` tool for the sake of simplicity, but an application uses etcd with the same API requests, storing, retrieving, and watching keys and ranges. The etcd Operator automates the etcd cluster part, making reliable key-value storage available to more applications.

Operators get considerably more complex, managing a variety of concerns, as you would expect from application-specific extensions. Nevertheless, most Operators follow the basic pattern discernable in the etcd Operator: a CR specifies some desired state, such as the version of an application, and a custom controller watches the resource, maintaining the desired state on the cluster.

You now have a Kubernetes cluster for working with Operators. You've seen how to deploy an Operator and triggered it to perform application-specific state reconciliation. Next, we'll introduce the Kubernetes API elements on which Operators build before introducing the Operator Framework and SDK, the toolkit you'll use to construct an Operator.

CHAPTER 3

Operators at the Kubernetes Interface

Operators extend two key Kubernetes concepts: *resources* and *controllers*. The Kubernetes API includes a mechanism, the CRD, for defining new resources. This chapter examines the Kubernetes objects Operators build on to add new capabilities to a cluster. It will help you understand how Operators fit into the Kubernetes architecture and why it is valuable to make an application a Kubernetes native.

Standard Scaling: The ReplicaSet Resource

Looking at a standard resource, the ReplicaSet, gives a sense of how resources comprise the application management database at the heart of Kubernetes. Like any other resource in the Kubernetes API, the ReplicaSet (*https://oreil.ly/nW3ui*) is a collection of API objects. The ReplicaSet primarily collects pod objects forming a list of the running replicas of an application. The specification of another object type defines the number of those replicas that should be maintained on the cluster. A third object spec points to a template for creating new pods when there are fewer running than desired. There are more objects collected in a ReplicaSet, but these three types define the basic state of a scalable set of pods running on the cluster. Here, we can see these three key pieces for the `staticweb` ReplicaSet from Chapter 1 (the `Selector`, `Replicas`, and `Pod Template` fields):

```
$ kubectl describe replicaset/staticweb-69ccd6d6c
Name:          staticweb-69ccd6d6c
Namespace:     default
Selector:      pod-template-hash=69ccd6d6c,run=staticweb
Labels:        pod-template-hash=69ccd6d6c
               run=staticweb
Controlled By: Deployment/staticweb
Replicas:      1 current / 1 desired
Pods Status:   1 Running / 0 Waiting / 0 Succeeded / 0 Failed
Pod Template:
```

```
Labels:    pod-template-hash=69ccd6d6c
           run=staticweb
Containers:
  staticweb:
    Image:          nginx
```

A standard Kubernetes control plane component, the ReplicaSet controller, manages ReplicaSets and the pods belonging to them. The ReplicaSet controller creates ReplicaSets and continually monitors them. When the count of running pods doesn't match the desired number in the `Replicas` field, the ReplicaSet controller starts or stops pods to make the actual state match the desired state.

The actions the ReplicaSet controller takes are intentionally general and application agnostic. It starts new replicas according to the pod template, or deletes excess pods. It does not, should not, and truly cannot know the particulars of startup and shutdown sequences for every application that might run on a Kubernetes cluster.

An Operator is the application-specific combination of CRs and a custom controller that does know all the details about starting, scaling, recovering, and managing its application. The Operator's *operand* is what we call the application, service, or whatever resources an Operator manages.

Custom Resources

CRs, as extensions of the Kubernetes API, contain one or more fields, like a native resource, but are not part of a default Kubernetes deployment. CRs hold structured data, and the API server provides a mechanism for reading and setting their fields as you would those in a native resource, by using `kubectl` or another API client. Users define a CR on a running cluster by providing a CR definition. A CRD is akin to a schema for a CR, defining the CR's fields and the types of values those fields contain.

CR or ConfigMap?

Kubernetes provides a standard resource, the *ConfigMap* (*https://oreil.ly/ba0uh*), for making configuration data available to applications. ConfigMaps seem to overlap with the possible uses for CRs, but the two abstractions target different cases.

ConfigMaps are best at providing a configuration to a program running in a pod on the cluster—think of an application's config file, like *httpd.conf* or MySQL's *mysql.cnf*. Applications usually want to read such configuration from within their pod, as a file or the value of an environment variable, rather than from the Kubernetes API.

Kubernetes provides CRs to represent new collections of objects in the API. CRs are created and accessed by standard Kubernetes clients, like `kubectl`, and they obey Kubernetes conventions, like the resources `.spec` and `.status`. At their most useful,

---

CRs are watched by custom controller code that in turn creates, updates, or deletes other cluster objects or even arbitrary resources outside of the cluster.

Custom Controllers

CRs are entries in the Kubernetes API database. They can be created, accessed, updated, and deleted with common kubectl commands—but a CR alone is merely a collection of data. To provide a declarative API for a specific application running on a cluster, you also need active code that captures the processes of managing that application.

We've looked at a standard Kubernetes controller, the ReplicaSet controller. To make an Operator, providing an API for the active management of an application, you build an instance of the Controller pattern to control your application. This custom controller checks and maintains the application's desired state, represented in the CR. Every Operator has one or more custom controllers implementing its application-specific management logic.

Operator Scopes

A Kubernetes cluster is divided into *namespaces*. A namespace is the boundary for cluster object and resource names. Names must be unique within a single namespace, but not between namespaces. This makes it easier for multiple users or teams to share a single cluster. Resource limits and access controls can be applied per namespace. An Operator, in turn, can be limited to a namespace, or it can maintain its operand across an entire cluster.

> For details about Kubernetes namespaces, see the Kubernetes namespace documentation (*https://oreil.ly/k4Okf*).

Namespace Scope

Usually, restricting your Operator to a single namespace makes sense and is more flexible for clusters used by multiple teams. An Operator scoped to a namespace can be upgraded independently of other instances, and this allows for some handy facilities. You can test upgrades in a testing namespace, for example, or serve older API or application versions from different namespaces for compatibility.

Cluster-Scoped Operators

There are some situations where it is desirable for an Operator to watch and manage an application or services throughout a cluster. For example, an Operator that manages a service mesh, such as Istio (*https://oreil.ly/jM5q2*), or one that issues TLS certificates for application endpoints, like `cert-manager` (*https://oreil.ly/QT8tE*), might be most effective when watching and acting on cluster-wide state.

By default, the Operator SDK used in this book creates deployment and authorization templates that limit the Operator to a single namespace. It is possible to change most Operators to run in the cluster scope instead. Doing so requires changes in the Operator's manifests to specify that it should watch all namespaces in a cluster and that it should run under the auspices of a ClusterRole and ClusterRoleBinding, rather than the namespaced Role and RoleBinding authorization objects. In the next section we give an overview of these concepts.

Authorization

Authorization—the power to do things on the cluster through the API—is defined in Kubernetes by one of a few available access control systems. Role-Based Access Control (RBAC) is the preferred and most tightly integrated of these. RBAC regulates access to system resources according to the *role* a system user performs. A role is a set of capabilities to take certain actions on particular API resources, such as *create*, *read*, *update*, or *delete*. The capabilities described by a role are granted, or bound, to a user by a RoleBinding.

Service Accounts

In Kubernetes, regular human user accounts aren't managed by the cluster, and there are no API resources depicting them. The user identifying you on the cluster comes from some outside provider, which can be anything from a list of users in a text file to an OpenID Connect (OIDC) provider proxying authentication through your Google account.

 See the "Users in Kubernetes" (*https://oreil.ly/WmdTq*) documentation for more about Kubernetes service accounts.

Service accounts, on the other hand, are managed by Kubernetes and can be created and manipulated through the Kubernetes API. A service account is a special type of cluster user for authorizing programs instead of people. An Operator is a program that uses the Kubernetes API, and most Operators should derive their access rights

---

from a service account. Creating a service account is a standard step in deploying an Operator. The service account identifies the Operator, and the account's role denotes the powers granted to the Operator.

Roles

Kubernetes RBAC denies permissions by default, so a role defines granted rights. A common "Hello World" example of a Kubernetes role looks something like this YAML excerpt:

```
apiVersion: rbac.authorization.k8s.io/v1
kind: Role
metadata:
  namespace: default
  name: pod-reader
rules:
- apiGroups: [""]
  resources: ["pods"]  ❶
  verbs: ["get", "watch", "list"]  ❷
```

❶ The powers granted by this role are effective only on pods.

❷ This list permits specific operations on the allowed resources. The verbs comprising read-only access to pods are available to accounts bound with this role.

RoleBindings

A RoleBinding ties a role to a list of one or more users. Those users are granted the permissions defined in the role referenced in the binding. A RoleBinding can reference only those roles in its own namespace. When deploying an Operator restricted to a namespace, a RoleBinding binds an appropriate role to a service account identifying the Operator.

ClusterRoles and ClusterRoleBindings

As discussed earlier, most Operators are confined to a namespace. Roles and Role-Bindings are also restricted to a namespace. ClusterRoles and ClusterRoleBindings are their cluster-wide equivalents. A standard, namespaced RoleBinding can reference only roles in its namespace, or ClusterRoles defined for the entire cluster. When a RoleBinding references a ClusterRole, the rules declared in the ClusterRole apply to only those specified resources in the binding's own namespace. In this way, a set of common roles can be defined once as ClusterRoles, but reused and granted to users in just a given namespace.

The ClusterRoleBinding grants capabilities to a user across the entire cluster, in all namespaces. Operators charged with cluster-wide responsibilities will often tie a ClusterRole to an Operator service account with a ClusterRoleBinding.

Summary

Operators are Kubernetes extensions. We've outlined the Kubernetes components used to construct an Operator that knows how to manage the application in its charge. Because Operators build on core Kubernetes concepts, they can make applications meaningfully "Kubernetes native." Aware of their environment, such applications are able to leverage not just the existing features but the design patterns of the platform in order to be more reliable and less needy. Because Operators politely extend Kubernetes, they can even manage parts and procedures of the platform itself, as seen throughout Red Hat's OpenShift Kubernetes distribution.

CHAPTER 4

The Operator Framework

There is inevitable complexity in developing an Operator, and in managing its distribution, deployment, and lifecycle. The Red Hat Operator Framework makes it simpler to create and distribute Operators. It makes building Operators easier with a software development kit (SDK) that automates much of the repetitive implementation work. The Framework also provides mechanisms for deploying and managing Operators. Operator Lifecycle Manager (OLM) is an Operator that installs, manages, and upgrades other Operators. Operator Metering is a metrics system that accounts for Operators' use of cluster resources. This chapter gives an overview of these three key parts of the Framework to prepare you to use those tools to build and distribute an example Operator. Along the way, you'll install the `operator-sdk` command-line tool, the primary interface to SDK features.

Operator Framework Origins

The Operator SDK builds atop the Kubernetes `controller-runtime` (*https://oreil.ly/AM0TP*), a set of libraries providing essential Kubernetes controller routines in the Go programming language. As part of the Operator Framework, the SDK provides integration points for distributing and managing Operators with OLM, and measuring them with Operator Metering. The SDK and the entire Red Hat Operator Framework are open source with contributors from throughout the community and other organizations, and are in the process of being donated (*https://oreil.ly/KoyS6*) to the vendor-neutral Cloud Native Computing Foundation (*https://www.cncf.io/*), home to Kubernetes itself and many other related projects.

Operator Maturity Model

The Operator Maturity Model, depicted in Figure 4-1, sketches a way to think about different levels of Operator functionality. You can begin with a minimum viable product that installs its operand, then add lifecycle management and upgrade capabilities, iterating over time toward complete automation for your application.

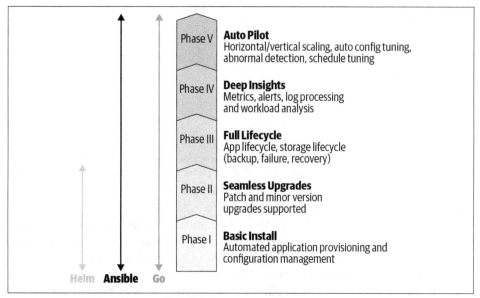

Figure 4-1. Operator Maturity Model

An Operator can have humble origins and grow in sophistication over a series of development cycles. The first phase of the model requires just enough application-specific code to create any resources the operand requires. In other words, phase one is the prepared, automated installation of an application.

Operator SDK

The Operator SDK (*https://oreil.ly/IcfRf*) is a set of tools for scaffolding, building, and preparing an Operator for deployment. The SDK currently includes first-class support for constructing Operators in the Go programming language, with support for other languages planned. The SDK also offers what might be described as an adapter architecture for Helm (*https://oreil.ly/IYH2d*) charts or Ansible (*https://oreil.ly/ek6jP*) playbooks. We'll cover these Adapter Operators in Chapter 6. In Chapter 7 we will show how to implement application-specific management routines in Go to build a custom Operator with the SDK tool.

Installing the Operator SDK Tool

The Operator SDK centers around a command-line tool, operator-sdk, that helps you build Operators. The SDK imposes a standard project layout, and in return creates skeletal Go source code for the basic Kubernetes API controller implementation and placeholders for your application-specific handlers. From there, the SDK provides convenience commands for building an Operator and wrapping it in a Linux container, generating the YAML-format Kubernetes manifests needed to deploy the Operator on Kubernetes clusters.

Binary installation

To install a binary for your operating system, download operator-sdk from the Kubernetes SDK repository (*https://oreil.ly/TTnC6*), make it executable, and move it into a directory in your $PATH. The program is statically linked, so it's ready to run on those platforms for which a release is available. At the time of this writing, the project supplies builds for macOS and Linux operating systems on the x86-64 architecture.

 With any rapidly evolving project like operator-sdk, it's a good idea to check the project's installation instructions (*https://oreil.ly/ ZbaBT*) for the latest installation method.

Installing from source

To get the latest development version, or for platforms with no binary distribution, build operator-sdk from source. We assume you have git and go installed:

```
$ go get -d github.com/operator-framework/operator-sdk
$ cd $GOPATH/src/github.com/operator-framework/operator-sdk
$ git checkout master
$ make tidy
$ make install
```

A successful build process writes the operator-sdk binary to your *$GOPATH/bin* directory. Run operator-sdk version to check it is in your $PATH.

These are the two most common and least dependent ways to get the SDK tool. Check the project's install documentation (*https://oreil.ly/fAC1b*) for other options. The subsequent examples in this book use version series 0.11.x of operator-sdk.

Operator Lifecycle Manager

Operators address the general principle that any application, on any platform, must be acquired, deployed, and managed over time. Operators are themselves Kubernetes applications. While an Operator manages its operand, what manages an Operator?

Operator Lifecycle Manager (*https://oreil.ly/SDL7q*) takes the Operator pattern one level up the stack: it's an Operator that acquires, deploys, and manages Operators on a Kubernetes cluster. Like an Operator for any application, OLM extends Kubernetes by way of custom resources and custom controllers so that Operators, too, can be managed declaratively, with Kubernetes tools, in terms of the Kubernetes API.

OLM defines a schema for Operator metadata, called the Cluster Service Version (CSV), for describing an Operator and its dependencies. Operators with a CSV can be listed as entries in a *catalog* available to OLM running on a Kubernetes cluster. Users then *subscribe* to an Operator from the catalog to tell OLM to provision and manage a desired Operator. That Operator, in turn, provisions and manages its application or service on the cluster.

Based on the description and parameters an Operator provides in its CSV, OLM can manage the Operator over its lifecycle: monitoring its state, taking actions to keep it running, coordinating among multiple instances on a cluster, and upgrading it to new versions. The Operator, in turn, can control its application with the latest automation features for the app's latest versions.

Operator Metering

Operator Metering is a system for analyzing the resource usage of the Operators running on Kubernetes clusters. Metering analyzes Kubernetes CPU, memory, and other resource metrics to calculate costs for infrastructure services. It can also examine application-specific metrics, such as those required to bill application users based on usage. Metering provides a model for ops teams to map the costs of a cloud service or a cluster resource to the application, namespace, and team consuming it. It's a platform atop which you can build customized reporting specific to your Operator and the application it manages, helping with three primary activities:

Budgeting
> When using Operators on their clusters, teams can gain insight into how infrastructure resources are used, especially in autoscaled clusters or hybrid cloud deployments, helping improve projections and allocations to avoid waste.

Billing
> When you build an Operator that provides a service to paying customers, resource usage can be tracked by billing codes or labels that reflect the internal structure of an Operator and application to calculate accurate and itemized bills.

Metrics aggregation
> Service usage and metrics can be viewed across namespaces or teams. For example, it can help you analyze the resources consumed by a PostgreSQL database Operator running many database server clusters and very many databases for different teams sharing a large Kubernetes cluster.

Summary

This chapter introduced the three pillars of the Operator Framework: the Operator SDK for building and developing Operators; Operator Lifecycle Manager for distributing, installing, and upgrading them; and Operator Metering for measuring Operator performance and resource consumption. Together these framework elements support the process of making an Operator and keeping it running.

You also installed the `operator-sdk` tool, so you're equipped with the primary tool for building Operators. To get started, we'll first introduce the example application you will construct an Operator to manage, the Visitors Site.

CHAPTER 5

Sample Application: Visitors Site

Real, production-level applications are difficult. Container-based architectures are often made up of multiple services, each requiring their own configuration and installation process. Maintaining these types of applications, including the individual components and their interactions, is a time-consuming and error-prone process. Operators are designed to reduce the difficulty in this process.

A simple, one–container "Hello World" application isn't going to provide enough complexity to fully demonstrate what Operators can do. To really help you understand the capabilities of Operators, we need an application that requires multiple Kubernetes resources with configuration values that cross between them to use for demonstration.

In this chapter we introduce the Visitors Site application, which we will use as an example in the following chapters that cover writing Operators. We'll take a look at the application architecture and how to run the site, as well as the process of installing it through traditional Kubernetes manifests. In the chapters that follow, we'll create Operators to deploy this application using each of the approaches provided by the Operator SDK (Helm, Ansible, and Go), and explore the benefits and drawbacks of each.

Application Overview

The Visitors Site tracks information about each request to its home page. Each time the page is refreshed, an entry is stored with details about the client, backend server, and timestamp. The home page displays a list of the most recent visits (as shown in Figure 5-1).

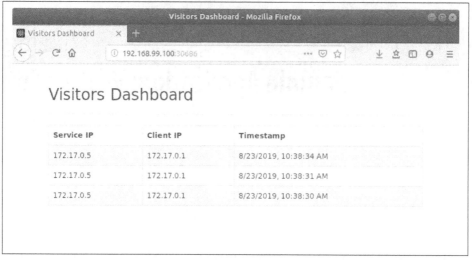

Figure 5-1. Visitors Site home page

While the home page itself is fairly simple, the architecture is what makes this an interesting example for exploring Operators. The Visitors Site is a traditional, three-tier application, consisting of:

- A web frontend, implemented in React (*https://reactjs.org/*)
- A REST API, implemented in Python (*https://www.python.org/*) using the Django framework (*https://www.djangoproject.com/*)
- A database, using MySQL (*https://www.mysql.com/*)

As shown in Figure 5-2, each of these components is deployed as a separate container. The flow is simple, with users interacting with the web interface, which itself makes calls to the backend REST API. The data submitted to the REST API is persisted in a MySQL database, which also runs as its own container.

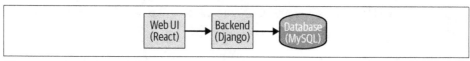

Figure 5-2. Visitors Site architecture

Note that the database does not connect to a persistent volume and stores its data ephemerally. While this isn't a suitable production solution, for the purposes of this example the important aspects are the deployments and interactions between the containers themselves.

Installation with Manifests

Each component in the Visitors Site requires two Kubernetes resources:

Deployment
> Contains the information needed to create the containers, including the image name, exposed ports, and specific configuration for a single deployment.

Service
> A network abstraction across all containers in a deployment. If a deployment is scaled up beyond one container, which we will do with the backend, the service sits in front and balances incoming requests across all of the replicas.

A third resource is used to store the authentication details for the database. The MySQL container uses this *secret* when it is started, and the backend containers use it to authenticate against the database when making requests.

Additionally, there are configuration values that must be consistent between components. For example, the backend needs to know the name of the database service to connect to. When deploying applications through manifests, awareness of these relationships is required to ensure that the values line up.

In the following manifests, the provided values will produce a working Visitors Site deployment. Each section will highlight specific instances where user intervention was required.

You can find all of the manifests in the book's GitHub repository (*https://github.com/ kubernetes-operators-book/chapters/tree/master/ch05*).

Deploying MySQL

The secret must be created before the database is deployed, since it is used during the container startup:

```
apiVersion: v1
kind: Secret
metadata:
  name: mysql-auth ❶
type: Opaque
stringData:
  username: visitors-user ❷
  password: visitors-pass ❷
```

❶ When the database and backend deployments use the secret, it is referred to by this name.

❷ For simplicity in this example, the username and password are defaulted to testing values.

You can find the definition for the secret resource in the *database.yaml* file in this book's GitHub repository (*https://oreil.ly/jZTgt*).

Once the secret is in place, use the following manifest to deploy a MySQL instance into Kubernetes:

```yaml
apiVersion: apps/v1
kind: Deployment
metadata:
  name: mysql  ❶
spec:
  replicas: 1
  selector:
    matchLabels:
      app: visitors
      tier: mysql
  template:
    metadata:
      labels:
        app: visitors
        tier: mysql
    spec:
      containers:
        - name: visitors-mysql
          image: "mysql:5.7"  ❷
          imagePullPolicy: Always
          ports:
            - name: mysql
              containerPort: 3306  ❸
              protocol: TCP
          env:  ❹
            - name: MYSQL_ROOT_PASSWORD
              value: password
            - name: MYSQL_DATABASE
              value: visitors_db
            - name: MYSQL_USER
              valueFrom:
                secretKeyRef:
                  name: mysql-auth  ❺
                  key: username
            - name: MYSQL_PASSWORD
              valueFrom:
                secretKeyRef:
                  name: mysql-auth  ❺
                  key: password
```

❶ The deployment name must be unique to the namespace in which it is deployed.

❷ The deployment requires the details of the image to deploy, including its name and hosting repository.

❸ Users must be aware of each port that the image exposes, and must explicitly reference them.

❹ The values used to configure the containers for this specific deployment are passed as environment variables.

❺ The secret provides the values for the database authentication credentials.

Keep in mind the value of the container port, as well as each of the environment variables, as other manifests use these values.

The deployment causes the creation of the MySQL container; however, it does not provide any ingress configuration on how to access it. For that, we will need a service. The following manifest will create a Kubernetes service that provides access to the MySQL deployment:

```
apiVersion: v1
kind: Service
metadata:
  name: mysql-service  ❶
  labels:
    app: visitors
    tier: mysql
spec:
  clusterIP: None
  ports:
    - port: 3306  ❷
  selector:
    app: visitors
    tier: mysql
```

❶ As with deployments, service names must be unique in a given namespace. This will also apply to the deployment and services for the backend and frontend components.

❷ The service maps to a port exposed by a deployment, so this value must be the same as in the `ports` section of the deployment.

Backend

Similar to the MySQL resources, the backend needs both a deployment and a service. However, whereas the database is standalone, the configuration for the backend relies heavily on the values set for the database. While this isn't an unreasonable requirement, it falls on the user to ensure that the values are consistent across both resources. A single error could result in the backend not being able to communicate with the database. Here's the manifest to deploy the backend:

```
apiVersion: apps/v1
kind: Deployment
metadata:
  name: visitors-backend
spec:
  replicas: 1   ❶
  selector:
    matchLabels:
      app: visitors
      tier: backend
  template:
    metadata:
      labels:
        app: visitors
        tier: backend
    spec:
      containers:
        - name: visitors-backend
          image: "jdob/visitors-service:1.0.0"
          imagePullPolicy: Always
          ports:
            - name: visitors
              containerPort: 8000
          env:
            - name: MYSQL_DATABASE   ❷
              value: visitors_db
            - name: MYSQL_SERVICE_HOST   ❸
              value: mysql-service
            - name: MYSQL_USERNAME
              valueFrom:
                secretKeyRef:
                  name: mysql-auth   ❹
                  key: username
            - name: MYSQL_PASSWORD
              valueFrom:
                secretKeyRef:
                  name: mysql-auth   ❹
                  key: password
```

❶ Each deployment configuration includes the number of containers it should spawn.

❷ These values must be manually checked to ensure they match up with the values set on the MySQL deployment. Otherwise, the backend will not be able to establish a connection to the database.

❸ This value tells the backend where to find the database and must match the name of the MySQL service created previously.

❹ As with the database deployment, the secret provides the authentication credentials for the database.

One of the major benefits of using containerized applications is the ability they give you to individually scale specific components. In the backend deployment shown here, the `replicas` field can be modified to scale the backend. The example Operators in the following chapters use a custom resource to expose this replica count as a first-class configuration value of the Visitors Site custom resource. Users do not need to manually navigate to the specific backend deployment as they do when using manifests. The Operator knows how to appropriately use the entered value.

The service manifest looks similar to the one you created for the database:

```
apiVersion: v1
kind: Service
metadata:
  name: visitors-backend-service
  labels:
    app: visitors
    tier: backend
spec:
  type: NodePort
  ports:
    - port: 8000      ❶
      targetPort: 8000
      nodePort: 30685  ❷
      protocol: TCP
  selector:
    app: visitors
    tier: backend
```

❶ As with the database service, the port referenced in the service definition must match up with that exposed by the deployment.

❷ In this example, the backend is configured to run through port 30685 on the same IP as Minikube. The frontend uses this port when making backend calls for data. For simplicity, the frontend defaults to using this value, so it does not need to be specified when the frontend is deployed.

Frontend

The frontend is in a similar position as the backend in the sense that it needs configuration that is consistent with the backend deployment. Once again, it falls on the user to manually verify that these values are consistent in both locations. Here's the manifest that creates the frontend deployment:

```
apiVersion: apps/v1
kind: Deployment
metadata:
  name: visitors-frontend
spec:
  replicas: 1
  selector:
    matchLabels:
      app: visitors
      tier: frontend
  template:
    metadata:
      labels:
        app: visitors
        tier: frontend
    spec:
      containers:
        - name: visitors-frontend
          image: "jdob/visitors-webui:1.0.0"
          imagePullPolicy: Always
          ports:
            - name: visitors
              containerPort: 3000
          env:
            - name: REACT_APP_TITLE  ❶
              value: "Visitors Dashboard"
```

❶ To make the Visitors Site application more interesting, you can override the home page title through an environment variable. The CR you'll learn how to create in the next chapters will expose it as a value of the Visitors Site, shielding end users from having to know in which deployment to specify the value.

Similar to the MySQL and backend deployments, the following manifest creates a service that provides access to the frontend deployment:

```
apiVersion: v1
kind: Service
metadata:
  name: visitors-frontend-service
  labels:
    app: visitors
    tier: frontend
spec:
  type: NodePort
  ports:
    - port: 3000
      targetPort: 3000
      nodePort: 30686  ❶
      protocol: TCP
  selector:
    app: visitors
    tier: frontend
```

➊ The frontend service looks very similar to the backend service, with the notable difference that it runs on port 30686.

Deploying the Manifests

You can run the Visitors Site for yourself using the kubectl command:

```
$ kubectl apply -f ch05/database.yaml
secret/mysql-auth created
deployment.apps/mysql created
service/mysql-service created

$ kubectl apply -f ch05/backend.yaml
deployment.apps/visitors-backend created
service/visitors-backend-service created

$ kubectl apply -f ch05/frontend.yaml
deployment.apps/visitors-frontend created
service/visitors-frontend-service created
```

Accessing the Visitors Site

Using these manifests, you can find the home page by using the IP address of the Minikube instance and specifying port 30686 in your browser. The minikube command provides the IP address to access:

```
$ minikube ip
192.168.99.100
```

For this Minikube instance, you can access the Visitors Site by opening a browser and going to *http://192.168.99.100:30686*.

Clicking refresh a few times will populate the table on that page with details of the internal cluster IP and the timestamp of each request, as previously shown in Figure 5-1.

Cleaning Up

Similar to deploying the manifests, you delete the created resources using the kubectl command:

```
$ kubectl delete -f ch05/frontend.yaml
deployment.apps "visitors-frontend" deleted
service "visitors-frontend-service" deleted

$ kubectl delete -f ch05/backend.yaml
deployment.apps "visitors-backend" deleted
service "visitors-backend-service" deleted
```

```
$ kubectl delete -f ch05/database.yaml
secret "mysql-auth" deleted
deployment.apps "mysql" deleted
service "mysql-service" deleted
```

Summary

We will use this sample application in the following chapters to demonstrate a variety of technologies on which you can build Operators.

In addition to the Operator implementations, keep in mind the end user experience. In this chapter we demonstrated a manifest-based installation, requiring a number of manual changes and internal references to be made. All of the following Operator implementations create a custom resource definition that acts as the sole API for creating and configuring an instance of the Visitors Site.

CHAPTER 6

Adapter Operators

Consider the numerous steps it would take to write an Operator from scratch. You would have to create CRDs to specify the interface for end users. Kubernetes controllers would not only need to be written with the Operator's domain-specific logic, but also be correctly hooked into a running cluster to receive the proper notifications. Roles and service accounts would need to be created to permit the Operator to function in the capacity it needs. An Operator is run as a pod inside of a cluster, so an image would need to be built, along with its accompanying deployment manifest.

Many projects have already invested in application deployment and configuration technologies. The Helm project allows users to define their cluster resources in a formatted text file and deploy them through the Helm command-line tools. Ansible is a popular automation engine for creating reusable scripts for provisioning and configuring a group of resources. Both projects have devoted followings of developers who may lack the resources to migrate to using Operators for their applications.

The Operator SDK provides a solution to both these problems through its *Adapter Operators*. Through the command-line tool, the SDK generates the code necessary to run technologies such as Helm and Ansible in an Operator. This allows you to rapidly migrate your infrastructure to an Operator model without needing to write the necessary supporting Operator code. The advantages of doing this include:

- Provides a consistent interface through CRDs, regardless of whether the underlying technology is Helm, Ansible, or Go.

- Allows the Helm and Ansible solutions to leverage the Operator deployment and lifecycle benefits that Operator Lifecycle Manager provides (see Chapter 8 for more information).

- Enables hosting of those solutions on Operator repositories like OperatorHub.io (see Chapter 10 for more information).

In this chapter we demonstrate how to use the SDK to build and test Adapter Operators using the Visitors Site application introduced in the previous chapter.

Custom Resource Definitions

Before we explain how to implement an Operator (in both this chapter and the next), it's important for you to understand the role of CRDs.

As discussed in Chapter 3, CRDs allow you to create domain-specific resources that correspond to your application. Using the standard Kubernetes APIs, end users interact with these resources to deploy and configure applications. Operators make heavy use of CRs and use *watches* on these objects to react to changes as they are made.

A CRD is the specification of what constitutes a CR. In particular, the CRD defines the allowed configuration values and the expected output that describes the current state of the resource.

In each of the following examples, both in this chapter and the next, a CRD is created when a new Operator project is generated by the SDK. The SDK prompts the user for two pieces of information about the CRD during project creation:

- The kind is the name of the CR type defined by the CRD. When creating new instances of this resource type, this value is used as the resource's kind field, similar to when creating a pod or service.

- The api-version contains information about the group and version of the CRD, which is specified when creating CRs according to that CRD schema. The value for this argument is specified in the format <group>/<version>, with the following recommendations:

  - The group should identify the organization that wrote and maintains the CRD. For example, the group for the EtcdCluster CR is etcd.database.coreos.com.

  - The version should follow the Kubernetes API versioning conventions (*https://oreil.ly/tk1hc*). For example, at the time of writing, the EtcdCluster version is v1beta2.

To recreate the EtcdCluster example, this api-version value is valid for the SDK:

```
--api-version=etcd.database.coreos.com/v1beta2
```

The kind and api-version of a CR are used when creating Operators of all types.

Helm Operator

Helm (*https://helm.sh/*) is a package manager for Kubernetes. It makes it easier to deploy applications with multiple components, but each deployment is still a manual process. If you're deploying many instances of a Helm-packaged app, it would be convenient to automate those deployments with an Operator.

Helm's intricacies are outside the scope of this book—you can consult the documentation (*https://helm.sh/docs/*) for more details—but a little background will help you understand the Helm Operator. Helm defines the Kubernetes resources that constitute an application, such as deployments and services, in a file called a *chart*. Charts support configuration variables, so you can customize application instances without needing to edit the chart itself. These configuration values are specified in a file named *values.yaml*. A Helm Operator can deploy each instance of an application with a different version of *values.yaml*.

The Operator SDK generates Kubernetes controller code for a Helm Operator when it is passed the `--type=helm` argument. You supply a Helm chart for your application, and the resulting Helm Operator watches for new CRs of its given type. When it finds one of these CRs, it constructs a Helm *values.yaml* file from the values defined in the resource. The Operator then creates the application resources specified in its Helm chart according to the settings in *values.yaml*. To configure another instance of the application, you create a new CR containing appropriate values for the instance.

The SDK provides two variations on how to build Helm-based Operators:

- The project generation process builds a blank Helm chart structure within the Operator project code.
- An existing chart is specified at Operator creation time, which the creation process uses to populate the generated Operator.

In the following sections we discuss each of these approaches. As a prerequisite, be sure to install the Helm command-line tools on your machine. You can find information on doing this in Helm's install documentation (*https://oreil.ly/qpZX0*).

Building the Operator

The SDK's `new` command creates the skeleton project files for a new Operator. These files include all of the code necessary for a Kubernetes controller that invokes the appropriate Helm chart to field requests for CRs. We'll discuss these files in greater detail later in this section.

Creating a new chart

To create an Operator with the skeleton for a new Helm chart, use the `--type=helm` argument. The following example creates the basis of a Helm Operator for the Visitors Site application (see Chapter 5):

```
$ OPERATOR_NAME=visitors-helm-operator
$ operator-sdk new $OPERATOR_NAME --api-version=example.com/v1 \
  --kind=VisitorsApp --type=helm
INFO[0000] Creating new Helm operator 'visitors-helm-operator'.
INFO[0000] Created helm-charts/visitorsapp
INFO[0000] Generating RBAC rules
WARN[0000] The RBAC rules generated in deploy/role.yaml are based on
the chart's default manifest. Some rules may be missing for resources
that are only enabled with custom values, and some existing rules may
be overly broad. Double check the rules generated in deploy/role.yaml
to ensure they meet the operator's permission requirements.
INFO[0000] Created build/Dockerfile
INFO[0000] Created watches.yaml
INFO[0000] Created deploy/service_account.yaml
INFO[0000] Created deploy/role.yaml
INFO[0000] Created deploy/role_binding.yaml
INFO[0000] Created deploy/operator.yaml
INFO[0000] Created deploy/crds/example_v1_visitorsapp_crd.yaml
INFO[0000] Created deploy/crds/example_v1_visitorsapp_cr.yaml
INFO[0000] Project creation complete.
```

`visitors-helm-operator` is the name of the generated Operator. The other two arguments, `--api-version` and `--kind`, describe the CR this Operator manages. These arguments result in the creation of a basic CRD for the new type.

The SDK creates a new directory with the same name as $OPERATOR_NAME, which contains all of the Operator's files. There are a few files and directories to note:

deploy/
> This directory contains Kubernetes template files that are used to deploy and configure the Operator, including the CRD, the Operator deployment resource itself, and the necessary RBAC resources for the Operator to run.

helm-charts/
> This directory contains a skeleton directory structure for a Helm chart with the same name as the CR kind. The files within are similar to those the Helm CLI creates when it initializes a new chart, including a *values.yaml* file. A new chart is added to this directory for each new CR type the Operator manages.

watches.yaml
> This file maps each CR type to the specific Helm chart that is used to handle it.

At this point, everything is in place to begin to implement your chart. However, if you already have a chart written, there is an easier approach.

Use an existing chart

The process for building an Operator from an existing Helm chart is similar to that for creating an Operator with a new chart. In addition to the `--type=helm` argument, there are a few additional arguments to take into consideration:

--helm-chart
  Tells the SDK to initialize the Operator with an existing chart. The value can be:

  - A URL to a chart archive

  - The repository and name of a remote chart

  - The location of a local directory

--helm-chart-repo
  Specifies a remote repository URL for the chart (unless a local directory is otherwise specified).

--helm-chart-version
  Tells the SDK to fetch a specific version of the chart. If this is omitted, the latest available version is used.

When using the `--helm-chart` argument, the `--api-version` and `--kind` arguments become optional. The `api-version` is defaulted to `charts.helm.k8s.io/v1alpha1` and the `kind` name will be derived from the name of the chart. However, as the `api-version` carries information about the CR creator, we recommend that you explicitly populate these values appropriately. You can find an example Helm chart for deploying the Visitors Site application in this book's GitHub repository (*https://github.com/kubernetes-operators-book/chapters/tree/master/ch06/visitors-helm*).

The following example demonstrates how to build an Operator and initialize it using an archive of the Visitors Site Helm chart:

```
$ OPERATOR_NAME=visitors-helm-operator
$ wget https://github.com/kubernetes-operators-book/\
  chapters/releases/download/1.0.0/visitors-helm.tgz   ❶
$ operator-sdk new $OPERATOR_NAME --api-version=example.com/v1 \
  --kind=VisitorsApp --type=helm --helm-chart=./visitors-helm.tgz
INFO[0000] Creating new Helm operator 'visitors-helm-operator'.
INFO[0000] Created helm-charts/visitors-helm
INFO[0000] Generating RBAC rules
WARN[0000] The RBAC rules generated in deploy/role.yaml are based on
the chart's default manifest. Some rules may be missing for resources
that are only enabled with custom values, and some existing rules may
be overly broad. Double check the rules generated in deploy/role.yaml
to ensure they meet the operator's permission requirements.
INFO[0000] Created build/Dockerfile
INFO[0000] Created watches.yaml
INFO[0000] Created deploy/service_account.yaml
```

```
INFO[0000] Created deploy/role.yaml
INFO[0000] Created deploy/role_binding.yaml
INFO[0000] Created deploy/operator.yaml
INFO[0000] Created deploy/crds/example_v1_visitorsapp_crd.yaml
INFO[0000] Created deploy/crds/example_v1_visitorsapp_cr.yaml
INFO[0000] Project creation complete.
```

❶ Due to an issue with how the Operator SDK handles redirects, you must manually download the chart tarball and pass it as a local reference.

The preceding example generates the same files as in the case of creating an Operator with a new Helm chart, with the notable exception that the chart files are populated from the specified archive:

```
$ ls -l $OPERATOR_NAME/helm-charts/visitors-helm/templates
_helpers.tpl
auth.yaml
backend-deployment.yaml
backend-service.yaml
frontend-deployment.yaml
frontend-service.yaml
mysql-deployment.yaml
mysql-service.yaml
tests
```

The SDK uses the values in the chart's *values.yaml* file to populate the example CR template. For example, the Visitors Site Helm chart has the following *values.yaml* file:

```
$ cat $OPERATOR_NAME/helm-charts/visitors-helm/values.yaml
backend:
  size: 1

frontend:
  title: Helm Installed Visitors Site
```

The example CR generated by the SDK, found in the *deploy/crds* directory in the Operator project root directory, includes these same values in its spec section:

```
$ cat $OPERATOR_NAME/deploy/crds/example_v1_visitorsapp_cr.yaml
apiVersion: example.com/v1
kind: VisitorsApp
metadata:
  name: example-visitorsapp
spec:
  # Default values copied from <proj_dir>/helm-charts/visitors-helm/values.yaml

  backend:
    size: 1

  frontend:
    title: Helm Installed Visitors Site
```

Before running the chart, the Operator will map the values found in the custom resource's spec field to the *values.yaml* file.

Fleshing Out the CRD

The generated CRD does not include specific details of the value input and state values of the CR type. Appendix B describes the steps you should take to finish defining the CR.

Reviewing Operator Permissions

The generated deployment files include the role the Operator will use to connect to the Kubernetes API. By default, this role is extremely permissive. Appendix C talks about how to fine-tune the role definition to limit the Operator's permissions.

Running the Helm Operator

An Operator is delivered as a normal container image. However, during the development and testing cycle, it is often easier to skip the image creation process and simply run the Operator outside of the cluster. In this section we describe those steps (see Appendix A for information about running the Operator as a deployment inside the cluster). Run all the commands here from within the Operator project root directory:

1. Create a local watches file. The generated *watches.yaml* file refers to a specific path where the Helm chart is found. This path makes sense in the deployed Operator scenario; the image creation process takes care of copying the chart to the necessary location. This *watches.yaml* file is still required when running the Operator outside of the cluster, so you need to manually make sure your chart can be found at that location.

   The simplest approach is to copy the existing *watches.yaml* file, which is located in the root of the Operator project:

   ```
   $ cp watches.yaml local-watches.yaml
   ```

   In the *local-watches.yaml* file, edit the chart field to contain the full path of the chart on your machine. Remember the name of the local watches file; you will need it later when you start the Operator process.

2. Create the CRDs in the cluster using the kubectl command:

   ```
   $ kubectl apply -f deploy/crds/*_crd.yaml
   ```

3. Once you have finished creating the CRDs, start the Operator using the following SDK command:

   ```
   $ operator-sdk up local --watches-file ./local-watches.yaml
   INFO[0000] Running the operator locally.
   INFO[0000] Using namespace default.  ❶
   ```

❶ The Operator log messages will appear in this running process as it starts up and fields CR requests.

This command starts a running process that behaves in the same way the Operator would if you had deployed it as a pod inside the cluster. (We'll cover testing in more detail in "Testing an Operator" on page 59.)

Ansible Operator

Ansible (*https://www.ansible.com/*) is a popular management tool for automating the provisioning and configuration of commonly run tasks. Similar to a Helm chart, an Ansible *playbook* defines a series of *tasks* that are run on a set of servers. Reusable *roles*, which extend Ansible through custom functionality, may be used to enhance the set of tasks in a playbook.

One useful collection of roles is k8s (*https://oreil.ly/1ckgw*), which provides tasks for interacting with a Kubernetes cluster. Using this module, you can write playbooks to handle the deployment of applications, including all of the necessary supporting Kubernetes resources.

The Operator SDK provides a way to build an Operator that will run Ansible playbooks to react to CR changes. The SDK supplies the code for the Kubernetes pieces, such as the controller, allowing you to focus on writing the playbooks themselves.

Building the Operator

As with its Helm support, the Operator SDK generates a project skeleton. When run with the --type=ansible argument, the project skeleton contains the structure for a blank Ansible role. The name of the role is derived from the specified CR type name.

The following example demonstrates creating an Ansible Operator that defines a CR for the Visitors Site application:

```
$ OPERATOR_NAME=visitors-ansible-operator
$ operator-sdk new $OPERATOR_NAME --api-version=example.com/v1 \
  --kind=VisitorsApp --type=ansible
INFO[0000] Creating new Ansible operator 'visitors-ansible-operator'.
INFO[0000] Created deploy/service_account.yaml
INFO[0000] Created deploy/role.yaml
INFO[0000] Created deploy/role_binding.yaml
INFO[0000] Created deploy/crds/example_v1_visitorsapp_crd.yaml
INFO[0000] Created deploy/crds/example_v1_visitorsapp_cr.yaml
INFO[0000] Created build/Dockerfile
INFO[0000] Created roles/visitorsapp/README.md
INFO[0000] Created roles/visitorsapp/meta/main.yml
INFO[0000] Created roles/visitorsapp/files/.placeholder
INFO[0000] Created roles/visitorsapp/templates/.placeholder
```

```
INFO[0000] Created roles/visitorsapp/vars/main.yml
INFO[0000] Created molecule/test-local/playbook.yml
INFO[0000] Created roles/visitorsapp/defaults/main.yml
INFO[0000] Created roles/visitorsapp/tasks/main.yml
INFO[0000] Created molecule/default/molecule.yml
INFO[0000] Created build/test-framework/Dockerfile
INFO[0000] Created molecule/test-cluster/molecule.yml
INFO[0000] Created molecule/default/prepare.yml
INFO[0000] Created molecule/default/playbook.yml
INFO[0000] Created build/test-framework/ansible-test.sh
INFO[0000] Created molecule/default/asserts.yml
INFO[0000] Created molecule/test-cluster/playbook.yml
INFO[0000] Created roles/visitorsapp/handlers/main.yml
INFO[0000] Created watches.yaml
INFO[0000] Created deploy/operator.yaml
INFO[0000] Created .travis.yml
INFO[0000] Created molecule/test-local/molecule.yml
INFO[0000] Created molecule/test-local/prepare.yml
INFO[0000] Project creation complete.
```

This command produces a similar directory structure to the Helm Operator example. The SDK creates a *deploy* directory that contains the same set of files, including the CRD and deployment template.

There are a few notable differences from the Helm Operator:

watches.yaml
- The purpose of this is the same as for the Helm Operator: it maps a CR type to the location of a file that is executed during its resolution. The Ansible Operator, however, supports two different types of files (these fields are mutually exclusive):
  - If the role field is included, it must point to the directory of an Ansible *role* that is executed during resource reconciliation.
  - If the playbook field is included, it must point to a *playbook* file that is run.
- The SDK defaults this file to point to the role it created during generation.

roles/
- This directory contains all of the Ansible roles that may be run by the Operator. The SDK generates the base files for a new role when the project is created.
- If the Operator manages multiple CR types, multiple roles are added to this directory. Additionally, an entry for each type, and its associated role, is added to the watches file.

Next, you'll implement the Ansible role for the CR. The details of what the role does will vary depending on the application: some common tasks include the creation of deployments and services to run the application's containers. For more on writing Ansible roles, see the Ansible documentation (*https://oreil.ly/bLd5g*).

You can find the Ansible role for deploying the Visitors Site in the book's GitHub repository (*https://github.com/kubernetes-operators-book/chapters/tree/master/ch06/ansible/visitors*). For simplicity while following along with the example application, the role files are available as a release there. Similar to the previous Operator creation command, you can add the Visitors Site role with the following:

```
$ cd $OPERATOR_NAME/roles/visitorsapp
$ wget https://github.com/kubernetes-operators-book/\
  chapters/releases/download/1.0.0/visitors-ansible.tgz
$ tar -zxvf visitors-ansible.tgz ❶
$ rm visitors-ansible.tgz
```

❶ This command overwrites the default generated role files with the files necessary to run the Visitors Site role.

We don't cover writing Ansible roles in this book, but it's important for you to understand how user-entered configuration values are propagated into an Ansible role.

As with the Helm Operator, configuration values come from the CR's `spec` section. However, within the playbooks and roles, Ansible's standard `{{ variable_name }}` syntax is used. Field names in Kubernetes typically use camel case (e.g., camelCase), so the Ansible Operator will convert the name of each field to snake case (e.g., snake_case) before passing the parameter to the Ansible role. That is, the field name `serviceAccount` would be converted to `service_account`. This allows the reuse of existing roles using the standard Ansible convention while also honoring the Kubernetes resource conventions. You can find the source for an Ansible role that deploys the Visitors Site in the book's GitHub repository (*https://github.com/kubernetes-operators-book/chapters/tree/master/ch06/ansible*).

Fleshing Out the CRD

As with the Helm Operator, you'll need to expand on the generated CRD to include the specifics of your CR. Consult Appendix B for more information.

Reviewing Operator Permissions

The Ansible Operator also includes a generated role the Operator uses to connect to the Kubernetes API. Check Appendix C for more on refining the default permissions.

Running the Ansible Operator

As with the Helm Operator, the easiest way to test and debug an Ansible Operator is to run it outside a cluster, avoiding the steps of building and pushing an image.

Before you can do this, however, there are a few extra steps you need to take:

1. First, install Ansible on the machine running the Operator. Consult the Ansible documentation (*https://oreil.ly/9yZRC*) for specifics on how to install Ansible on your local OS.

2. Additional Ansible-related packages must be installed as well, including the following (consult the documentation for details on installation):

   - Ansible Runner (*https://oreil.ly/lHDCe*)

   - Ansible Runner HTTP Event Emitter (*https://oreil.ly/N6ebi*)

3. As with the Helm Operator, the *watches.yaml* file generated by the SDK refers to a specific directory for the Ansible role. So you'll copy the watches file and modify it as necessary. Again, run these commands from within the Operator project root directory:

   ```
   $ cp watches.yaml local-watches.yaml
   ```

   In the *local-watches.yaml* file, change the `role` field to reflect the directory structure on your machine.

4. Create the CRDs in the cluster using the `kubectl` command:

   ```
   $ kubectl apply -f deploy/crds/*_crd.yaml
   ```

5. Once the CRDs are deployed in the cluster, run the Operator using the SDK:

   ```
   $ operator-sdk up local --watches-file ./local-watches.yaml
   INFO[0000] Running the operator locally.
   INFO[0000] Using namespace default. ❶
   ```

   ❶ The Operator log messages will appear in this running process as it starts up and fields CR requests.

   This command starts a running process that behaves as the Operator would if it was deployed as a pod inside the cluster.

Now let's walk through the steps of how to test an Operator.

Testing an Operator

You can test both of the Adapter Operators using the same approach: by deploying a CR. Kubernetes notifies the Operator of the CR, which then executes the underlying files (either Helm charts or Ansible roles). The SDK generates a sample CR template in the *deploy/crds* directory that you can use, or you can create one manually.

Follow these steps to test both types of Operators discussed in this chapter:

1. Edit the `spec` section of the example CR template (in the Visitors Site example, this is named *example_v1_visitorsapp_cr.yaml*) with whatever values are relevant to your CR.

2. Create the resource (in the Operator project root directory) using the Kubernetes CLI:

```
$ kubectl apply -f deploy/crds/*_cr.yaml
```

The output for the Operator will appear in the same terminal where you ran the `operator-sdk up local` command. Once the test is complete, end the running process by pressing `Ctrl-C`.

3. Navigate to the Visitors Site as described in Chapter 5 to verify the application works as expected.

4. Once the test is complete, delete the CR using the `kubectl delete` command:

```
$ kubectl delete -f deploy/crds/*_cr.yaml
```

During development, repeat this process to test changes. On each iteration, be sure to restart the Operator process to pick up any changes to the Helm or Ansible files.

Summary

You don't need to be a programmer to write an Operator. The Operator SDK facilitates the packaging of two existing provisioning and configuration technologies, Helm and Ansible, as Operators. The SDK also provides a way to rapidly test and debug changes by running an Operator outside of the cluster, skipping the time-consuming image building and hosting steps.

In the next chapter, we'll look at a more powerful and flexible way of implementing Operators by using the Go language.

Resources

- Helm (*https://helm.sh/*)
- Ansible (*https://www.ansible.com/*)
- Example Operators (*https://oreil.ly/KbPFs*)

CHAPTER 7

Operators in Go with the Operator SDK

While the Helm and Ansible Operators can be created quickly and easily, their functionality is ultimately limited by those underlying technologies. Advanced use cases, such as those that involve dynamically reacting to specific changes in the application or the cluster as a whole, require a more flexixble solution.

The Operator SDK provides that flexibility by making it easy for developers to use the Go programming language, including its ecosystem of external libraries, in their Operators.

As the process is slightly more involved than for the Helm or Ansible Operators, it makes sense to start with a summary of the high–level steps:

1. Create the necessary code that will tie in to Kubernetes and allow it to run the Operator as a controller.

2. Create one or more CRDs to model the application's underlying business logic and provide the API for users to interact with.

3. Create a controller for each CRD to handle the lifecycle of its resources.

4. Build the Operator image and create the accompanying Kubernetes manifests to deploy the Operator and its RBAC components (service accounts, roles, etc.).

While you can write all these pieces manually, the Operator SDK provides commands that will automate the creation of much of the supporting code, allowing you to focus on implementing the actual business logic of the Operator.

This chapter uses the Operator SDK to build the project skeleton for implementing an Operator in Go (see Chapter 4 for instructions on the SDK installation). We will explore the files that need to be edited with custom application logic and discuss some common practices for Operator development. Once the Operator is ready, we'll run it in development mode for testing and debugging.

Initializing the Operator

Since the Operator is written in Go, the project skeleton must adhere to the language conventions. In particular, the Operator code must be located in your $GOPATH. See the GOPATH documentation (*https://oreil.ly/2PU_Q*) for more information.

The SDK's new command creates the necessary base files for the Operator. If a specific Operator type is not specified, the command generates a Go-based Operator project:

```
$ OPERATOR_NAME=visitors-operator
$ operator-sdk new $OPERATOR_NAME
INFO[0000] Creating new Go operator 'visitors-operator'.
INFO[0000] Created go.mod
INFO[0000] Created tools.go
INFO[0000] Created cmd/manager/main.go
INFO[0000] Created build/Dockerfile
INFO[0000] Created build/bin/entrypoint
INFO[0000] Created build/bin/user_setup
INFO[0000] Created deploy/service_account.yaml
INFO[0000] Created deploy/role.yaml
INFO[0000] Created deploy/role_binding.yaml
INFO[0000] Created deploy/operator.yaml
INFO[0000] Created pkg/apis/apis.go
INFO[0000] Created pkg/controller/controller.go
INFO[0000] Created version/version.go
INFO[0000] Created .gitignore
INFO[0000] Validating project
[...] ❶
```

❶ The output is truncated for readability. The generation can take a few minutes as all of the Go dependencies are downloaded. The details of these dependencies will appear in the command output.

The SDK creates a new directory with the same name as $OPERATOR_NAME. The generation process produces hundreds of files, both generated and vendor files, that the Operator uses. Conveniently, you do not need to manually edit most of them. We will show you how to generate the files necessary to fulfill custom logic for an Operator in "Custom Resource Definitions" on page 64.

Operator Scope

One of the first decisions you need to make is the scope of the Operator. There are two options:

Namespaced
> Limits the Operator to managing resources in a single namespace

Cluster
> Allows the Operator to manage resources across the entire cluster

By default, Operators that the SDK generates are namespace-scoped.

While namespace-scoped Operators are often preferable, changing an SDK–generated Operator to be cluster-scoped is possible. Make the following changes to enable the Operator to work at the cluster level:

deploy/operator.yaml
- Change the value of the `WATCH_NAMESPACE` variable to `""`, indicating all namespaces will be watched instead of only the namespace in which the Operator pod is deployed.

deploy/role.yaml
- Change the `kind` from `Role` to `ClusterRole` to enable permissions outside of the Operator pod's namespace.

deploy/role_binding.yaml
- Change the `kind` from `RoleBinding` to `ClusterRoleBinding`.
- Under `roleRef`, change the `kind` to `ClusterRole`.
- Under `subjects`, add the key `namespace` with the value being the namespace in which the Operator pod is deployed.

Additionally, you need to update the generated CRDs (discussed in the following section) to indicate that the definition is cluster-scoped:

- In the `spec` section of the CRD file, change the `scope` field to `Cluster` instead of the default value of `Namespaced`.
- In the *_types.go* file for the CRD, add the tag `// +genclient:nonNamespaced` above the struct for the CR (this will have the same name as the `kind` field you used to create it). This ensures that future calls to the Operator SDK to refresh the CRD will not reset the value to the default.

For example, the following modifications to the `VisitorsApp` struct indicate that it is cluster-scoped:

```
// +k8s:deepcopy-gen:interfaces=k8s.io/apimachinery/pkg/runtime.Object

// VisitorsApp is the Schema for the visitorsapps API
// +k8s:openapi-gen=true
```

```
// +kubebuilder:subresource:status
// +genclient:nonNamespaced    ❶
type VisitorsApp struct {
```

❶ The tag must be before the resource type struct.

Custom Resource Definitions

In Chapter 6, we discussed the role of CRDs when creating an Operator. You can add new CRDs to an Operator using the SDK's add api command. This command, run from the Operator project root directory, generates the CRD for the Visitors Site example used in this book (using the arbitrary "example.com" for demonstration purposes):

```
$ operator-sdk add api --api-version=example.com/v1 --kind=VisitorsApp
INFO[0000] Generating api version example.com/v1 for kind VisitorsApp.
INFO[0000] Created pkg/apis/example/group.go
INFO[0000] Created pkg/apis/example/v1/visitorsapp_types.go
INFO[0000] Created pkg/apis/addtoscheme_example_v1.go
INFO[0000] Created pkg/apis/example/v1/register.go
INFO[0000] Created pkg/apis/example/v1/doc.go
INFO[0000] Created deploy/crds/example_v1_visitorsapp_cr.yaml
INFO[0001] Created deploy/crds/example_v1_visitorsapp_crd.yaml
INFO[0001] Running deepcopy code-generation for Custom Resource group versions:
  [example:[v1], ]
INFO[0001] Code-generation complete.
INFO[0001] Running OpenAPI code-generation for Custom Resource group versions:
  [example:[v1], ]
INFO[0003] Created deploy/crds/example_v1_visitorsapp_crd.yaml
INFO[0003] Code-generation complete.
INFO[0003] API generation complete.
```

The command generates a number of files. In the following list, note how both the api-version and CR type name (kind) contribute to the generated names (file paths are relative to the Operator project root):

deploy/crds/example_v1_visitorsapp-cr.yaml
> This is an example CR of the generated type. It is prepopulated with the appropriate api-version and kind, as well as a name for the resource. You'll need to fill out the spec section with values relevant to the CRD you created.

deploy/crds/example_v1_visitorsapp_crd.yaml
> This file is the beginning of a CRD manifest. The SDK generates many of the fields related to the name of the resource type (such as plural and list variations), but you'll need to add in the custom fields specific to your resource type. Appendix B goes into detail on fleshing out this file.

pkg/apis/example/v1/visitorsapp_types.go

This file contains a number of struct objects that the Operator codebase lever-ages. This file, unlike many of the generated Go files, is intended to be edited.

The `add api` command builds the appropriate skeleton code, but before you can use the resource type, you must define the set of configuration values that are specified when creating a new resource. You'll also need to add a description of the fields the CR will use when reporting its status. You'll add these sets of values in the definition template itself as well as the Go objects. The following two sections go into more detail about each step.

Defining the Go Types

In the **_types.go* file (in this example, *visitorsapp_types.go*), there are two struct objects that you need to address:

- The spec object (in this example, `VisitorsAppSpec`) must include all possible configuration values that may be specified for resources of this type. Each config-uration value is made up of the following:
  - The name of the variable as it will be referenced from within the Operator code (following Go conventions and beginning with a capital letter for lan-guage visibility purposes)
  - The Go type for the variable
  - The name of the field as it will be specified in the CR (in other words, the JSON or YAML manifest users will write to create the resource)
- The status object (in this example, `VisitorsAppStatus`) must include all possible values that the Operator may set to convey the state of the CR. Each value con-sists of the following:
  - The name of the variable as it will be referenced from within the Operator code (following Go conventions and beginning with a capital letter for visibil-ity purposes)
  - The Go type for the variable
  - The name of the field as it will appear in the description of the CR (for exam-ple, when getting the resource with the `-o yaml` flag)

The Visitors Site example supports the following values in its VisitorsApp CR:

`Size`
The number of backend replicas to create

`Title`
The text to display on the frontend web page

It is important to realize that despite the fact that you are using these values in differ-ent pods in the application, you are including them in a single CRD. From the end user's perspective, they are attributes of the overall application. It is the Operator's responsibility to determine how to use the values.

The VisitorsApp CR uses the following values in the status of each resource:

BackendImage
    Indicates the image and version used to deploy the backend pods

FrontendImage
    Indicates the image and version used to deploy the frontend pod

The following snippet from the *visitorsapp_types.go* file demonstrates these additions:

```
type VisitorsAppSpec struct {
    Size      int32  `json:"size"`
    Title     string `json:"title"`
}

type VisitorsAppStatus struct {
    BackendImage  string `json:"backendImage"`
    FrontendImage string `json:"frontendImage"`
}
```

The remainder of the *visitorsapp_types.go* file does not require any further changes.

After any change to a *_types.go* file, you need to update any generated code that works with these objects using the SDK's generate command (from the project's root directory):

```
$ operator-sdk generate k8s
INFO[0000] Running deepcopy code-generation for Custom Resource
group versions: [example:[v1], ]
INFO[0000] Code-generation complete.
```

The CRD Manifest

The additions to the types file are useful within the Operator code, but provide no insight to the end user creating the resource. Those additions are made to the CRD itself.

Similar to the types file, you'll make the additions to the CRD in the spec and status sections. Appendix B describes the process of editing these sections.

Operator Permissions

In addition to generating a CRD, the Operator SDK creates the RBAC resources the Operator needs to run. The generated role is extremely permissive by default, and you should refine its granted permissions before you deploy the Operator to production. Appendix C covers all of the RBAC-related files and talks about how to scope the permissions to what is applicable to the Operator.

Controller

The CRD and its associated types file in Go define the inbound API through which users will communicate. Inside of the Operator pod itself, you need a controller to watch for changes to CRs and react accordingly.

Similar to adding a CRD, you use the SDK to generate the controller's skeleton code. You'll use the api-version and kind of the previously generated resource definition to scope the controller to that type. The following snippet continues the Visitors Site example:

```
$ operator-sdk add controller --api-version=example.com/v1 --kind=VisitorsApp
INFO[0000] Generating controller version example.com/v1 for kind VisitorsApp.
INFO[0000] Created pkg/controller/visitorsapp/visitorsapp_controller.go  ❶
INFO[0000] Created pkg/controller/add_visitorsapp.go
INFO[0000] Controller generation complete.
```

❶ Note the name of this file. It contains the Kubernetes controller that implements the Operator's custom logic.

As with the CRD, this command generates a number of files. Of particular interest is the controller file, which is located and named according to the associated kind. You do not need to manually edit the other generated files.

The controller is responsible for "reconciling" a specific resource. The notion of a single reconcile operation is consistent with the declarative model that Kubernetes follows. Instead of having explicit handling for events such as add, delete, or update, the controller is passed the current state of the resource. It is up to the controller to determine the set of changes to update reality to reflect the desired state described in the resource. More information on Kubernetes controllers is found in the official Kubernetes documentation (*https://oreil.ly/E_hau*).

In addition to the reconcile logic, the controller also needs to establish one or more "watches." A watch indicates that Kubernetes should invoke this controller when changes to the "watched" resources occur. While the bulk of the Operator logic resides in the controller's Reconcile function, the add function establishes the watches that will trigger reconcile events. The SDK adds two such watches in the generated controller.

The first watch listens for changes to the primary resource that the controller monitors. The SDK generates this watch against resources of the same type as the kind parameter that was used when first generating the controller. In most cases, this does not need to be changed. The following snippet creates the watch for the VisitorsApp resource type:

```
// Watch for changes to primary resource VisitorsApp
err = c.Watch(&source.Kind{Type: &examplev1.VisitorsApp{}},
            &handler.EnqueueRequestForObject{})
if err != nil {
    return err
}
```

The second watch, or more accurately, series of watches, listens for changes to any child resources the Operator created to support the primary resource. For example, creating a VisitorsApp resource results in the creation of multiple deployment and service objects to support its function. The controller creates a watch for each of these child types, being careful to scope the watch to only child resources whose owner is of the same type as the primary resource. For example, the following code creates two watches, one for deployments and one for services whose parent resource is of the type VisitorsApp:

```
err = c.Watch(&source.Kind{Type: &appsv1.Deployment{}},
            &handler.EnqueueRequestForOwner{
    IsController: true,
    OwnerType:    &examplev1.VisitorsApp{},
})
if err != nil {
    return err
}

err = c.Watch(&source.Kind{Type: &corev1.Service{}},
            &handler.EnqueueRequestForOwner{
    IsController: true,
    OwnerType:    &examplev1.VisitorsApp{},
})
if err != nil {
    return err
}
```

For the watches created in this snippet, there are two areas of interest:

- The value for Type in the constructor indicates the child resource type that Kubernetes watches. Each child resource type needs its own watch.

- The watches for each of the child resource types set the value for OwnerType to the primary resource type, scoping the watch and causing Kubernetes to trigger a reconcile on the parent resource. Without this, Kubernetes will trigger a reconcile on this controller for *all* service and deployment changes, regardless of whether or not they belong to the Operator.

The Reconcile Function

The `Reconcile` function, also known as the *reconcile loop*, is where the Operator's logic resides. The purpose of this function is to resolve the actual state of the system against the desired state requested by the resource. More information to help you write this function is included in the next section.

 As Kubernetes invokes the `Reconcile` function multiple times throughout the lifecycle of a resource, it is important that the implementation be idempotent to prevent the creation of duplicate child resources. More information is found in "Idempotency" on page 75.

The `Reconcile` function returns two objects: a `ReconcileResult` instance and an error (if one is encountered). These return values indicate whether or not Kubernetes should requeue the request. In other words, the Operator tells Kubernetes if the reconcile loop should execute again. The possible outcomes based on the return values are:

`return reconcile.Result{}, nil`
> The reconcile process finished with no errors and does not require another pass through the reconcile loop.

`return reconcile.Result{}, err`
> The reconcile failed due to an error and Kubernetes should requeue it to try again.

`return reconcile.Result{Requeue: true}, nil`
> The reconcile did not encounter an error, but Kubernetes should requeue it to run for another iteration.

`return reconcile.Result{RequeueAfter: time.Second*5}, nil`
> Similar to the previous result, but this will wait for the specified amount of time before requeuing the request. This approach is useful when there are multiple steps that must run serially, but may take some time to complete. For example, if a backend service needs a running database prior to starting, the reconcile can be requeued with a delay to give the database time to start. Once the database is running, the Operator does not requeue the reconcile request, and the rest of the steps continue.

Operator Writing Tips

It is impossible to cover all of the conceivable uses and intricacies of Operators in a single book. The differences in application installation and upgrade alone are too many to enumerate, and those represent only the first two layers of the Operator Maturity Model. Instead, we will cover some general guidelines to get you started with the basic functions commonly performed by Operators.

Since Go-based Operators make heavy use of the Go Kubernetes libraries, it may be useful to review the API documentation (*https://godoc.org/k8s.io/api*). In particular, the core/v1 and apps/v1 modules are frequently used to interact with the common Kubernetes resources.

Retrieving the Resource

The first step the Reconcile function typically performs is to retrieve the primary resource that triggered the reconcile request. The Operator SDK generates the code for this, which should look similar to the following from the Visitors Site example:

```
// Fetch the VisitorsApp instance
instance := &examplev1.VisitorsApp{}
err := r.client.Get(context.TODO(), request.NamespacedName, instance) ❶❷

if err != nil {
    if errors.IsNotFound(err) {
        return reconcile.Result{}, nil ❸
    }
    // Error reading the object - requeue the request.
    return reconcile.Result{}, err
}
```

❶ Populates the previously created VisitorsApp object with the values from the resource that triggered the reconcile.

❷ The variable r is the reconciler object the Reconcile function is called on. It provides the client object, which is an authenticated client for the Kubernetes API.

❸ When a resource is deleted, Kubernetes still calls the Reconcile function, in which case the Get call returns an error. In this example, the Operator requires no further cleanup of deleted resources and simply returns that the reconcile was a success. We provide more information on handling deleted resources in "Child Resource Deletion" on page 74.

The retrieved instance serves two primary purposes:

- Retrieving configuration values about the resource from its Spec field

- Setting the current state of the resource using its `Status` field, and saving that updated information into Kubernetes

In addition to the `Get` function, the client provides a function to update a resource's values. When updating a resource's `Status` field, you'll use this function to persist the changes to the resource back into Kubernetes. The following snippet updates one of the fields in the previously retrieved VisitorsApp instance's status and saves the changes back into Kubernetes:

```
instance.Status.BackendImage = "example"
err := r.client.Status().Update(context.TODO(), instance)
```

Child Resource Creation

One of the first tasks commonly implemented in an Operator is to deploy the resources necessary to get the application running. It is critical that this operation be idempotent; subsequent calls to the `Reconcile` function should ensure the resource is running rather than creating duplicate resources.

These child resources commonly include, but are not limited to, deployment and service objects. The handling for them is similar and straightforward: check to see if the resource is present in the namespace and, if it is not, create it.

The following example snippet checks for the existence of a deployment in the target namespace:

```
found := &appsv1.Deployment{}
findMe := types.NamespacedName{
    Name:      "myDeployment",      ❶
    Namespace: instance.Namespace,  ❷
}
err := r.client.Get(context.TODO(), findMe, found)
if err != nil && errors.IsNotFound(err) {
    // Creation logic ❸
}
```

❶ The Operator knows the names of the child resources it created, or at least how to derive them (see "Child Resource Naming" on page 75 for a more in-depth discussion). In real use cases, `"myDeployment"` is replaced with the same name the Operator used when the deployment was created, taking care to ensure uniqueness relative to the namespace as appropriate.

❷ The `instance` variable was set in the earlier snippet about resource retrieval and refers to the object representing the primary resource being reconciled.

❸ At this point, the child resource was not found and no further errors were retrieved from the Kubernetes API, so the resource creation logic should be executed.

The Operator creates resources by populating the necessary Kubernetes objects and using the client to request that they be created. Consult the Kubernetes Go client API for specifications on how to instantiate the resource for each type. You'll find many of the desired specs in either the core/v1 or the apps/v1 module.

As an example, the following snippet creates a deployment specification for the MySQL database used in the Visitors Site example application:

```go
labels := map[string]string {
    "app":            "visitors",
    "visitorssite_cr": instance.Name,
    "tier":           "mysql",
}
size := int32(1)  ❶

userSecret := &corev1.EnvVarSource{
    SecretKeyRef: &corev1.SecretKeySelector{
        LocalObjectReference: corev1.LocalObjectReference{Name: mysqlAuthName()},
        Key: "username",
    },
}

passwordSecret := &corev1.EnvVarSource{
    SecretKeyRef: &corev1.SecretKeySelector{
        LocalObjectReference: corev1.LocalObjectReference{Name: mysqlAuthName()},
        Key: "password",
    },
}

dep := &appsv1.Deployment{
    ObjectMeta: metav1.ObjectMeta{
        Name:      "mysql-backend-service",  ❷
        Namespace: instance.Namespace,
    },
    Spec: appsv1.DeploymentSpec{
        Replicas: &size,
        Selector: &metav1.LabelSelector{
            MatchLabels: labels,
        },
        Template: corev1.PodTemplateSpec{
            ObjectMeta: metav1.ObjectMeta{
                Labels: labels,
            },
            Spec: corev1.PodSpec{
                Containers: []corev1.Container{{
                    Image: "mysql:5.7",
                    Name:  "visitors-mysql",
```

```
                    Ports:  []corev1.ContainerPort{{
                        ContainerPort:   3306,
                        Name:            "mysql",
                    }},
                    Env: []corev1.EnvVar{ ❸
                        {
                            Name: "MYSQL_ROOT_PASSWORD",
                            Value: "password",
                        },
                        {
                            Name: "MYSQL_DATABASE",
                            Value: "visitors",
                        },
                        {
                            Name: "MYSQL_USER",
                            ValueFrom: userSecret,
                        },
                        {
                            Name: "MYSQL_PASSWORD",
                            ValueFrom: passwordSecret,
                        },
                    },
                }},
            },
        },
    },
}

controllerutil.SetControllerReference(instance, dep, r.scheme) ❹
```

❶ In many cases, the Operator would read the number of deployed pods from the primary resource's spec. For simplicity, this is hardcoded to 1 in this example.

❷ This is the value used in the earlier snippet when you are attempting to see if the deployment exists.

❸ For this example, these are hardcoded values. Take care to generate randomized values as appropriate.

❹ This is, arguably, the most important line in the definition. It establishes the parent/child relationship between the primary resource (VisitorsApp) and the child (deployment). Kubernetes uses this relationship for certain operations, as you'll see in the following section.

The structure of the Go representation of the deployment closely resembles the YAML definition. Again, consult the API documentation for the specifics on how to use the Go object models.

Regardless of the child resource type (deployment, service, etc.), create it using the client:

```
createMe := // Deployment instance from above

// Create the service
err = r.client.Create(context.TODO(), createMe)

if err != nil {
    // Creation failed
    return &reconcile.Result{}, err
} else {
    // Creation was successful
    return nil, nil
}
```

Child Resource Deletion

In most cases, deleting child resources is significantly simpler than creating them: Kubernetes will do it for you. If the child resource's owner type is correctly set to the primary resource, when the parent is deleted, Kubernetes garbage collection will automatically clean up all of its child resources.

It is important to understand that when Kubernetes deletes a resource, it still calls the Reconcile function. Kubernetes garbage collection is still performed, and the Operator will not be able to retrieve the primary resource. See "Retrieving the Resource" on page 70 for an example of the code that checks for this situation.

There are times, however, where specific cleanup logic is required. The approach in such instances is to block the deletion of the primary resource through the use of a *finalizer*.

A finalizer is simply a series of strings on a resource. If one or more finalizers are present on a resource, the metadata.deletionTimestamp field of the object is populated, signifying the end user's desire to delete the resource. However, Kubernetes will only perform the actual deletion once all of the finalizers are removed.

Using this construct, you can block the garbage collection of a resource until the Operator has a chance to perform its own cleanup step. Once the Operator has finished with the necessary cleanup, it removes the finalizer, unblocking Kubernetes from performing its normal deletion steps.

The following snippet demonstrates using a finalizer to provide a window in which the Operator can take pre-deletion steps. This code executes after the retrieval of the instance object, as outlined in "Retrieving the Resource" on page 70:

```
finalizer := "visitors.example.com"

beingDeleted := instance.GetDeletionTimestamp() != nil  ❶
```

```
if beingDeleted {
    if contains(instance.GetFinalizers(), finalizer) {

        // Perform finalization logic. If this fails, leave the finalizer
        // intact and requeue the reconcile request to attempt the clean
        // up again without allowing Kubernetes to actually delete
        // the resource.

        instance.SetFinalizers(remove(instance.GetFinalizers(), finalizer)) ❷
        err := r.client.Update(context.TODO(), instance)
        if err != nil {
            return reconcile.Result{}, err
        }
    }
    return reconcile.Result{}, nil
}
```

❶ The presence of a deletion timestamp indicates that a requested delete is being blocked by one or more finalizers.

❷ Once the cleanup tasks have finished, the Operator removes the finalizer so Kubernetes can continue with the resource cleanup.

Child Resource Naming

While the end user provides the name of the CR when creating it, the Operator is responsible for generating the names of any child resources it creates. Take into consideration the following principles when creating these names:

- Resource names must be unique within a given namespace.
- Child resource names should be dynamically generated. Hardcoding child resource names leads to conflicts if there are multiple resources of the CR type in the same namespace.
- Child resource names must be reproducible and consistent. An Operator may need to access a resource's children in a future iteration through the reconcile loop and must be able to reliably retrieve those resources by name.

Idempotency

One of the biggest hurdles many developers face when writing controllers is the idea that Kubernetes uses a *declarative* API. End users don't issue commands that Kubernetes immediately fulfills. Instead, they request an end state that the cluster should achieve.

As such, the interface for controllers (and by extension, Operators) doesn't include imperative commands such as "add resource" or "change a configuration value."

Instead, Kubernetes simply asks the controller to reconcile the state of a resource. The Operator then determines what steps, if any, it will take to ensure that end state.

Therefore, it is critical that Operators are *idempotent*. Multiple calls to reconcile an unchanged resource must produce the same effect each time.

The following tips can help you ensure idempotency in your Operators:

- Before creating child resources, check to see if they already exist. Remember, Kubernetes may call the reconcile loop for a variety of reasons beyond when a user first creates a CR. Your controller should not duplicate the CR's children on each iteration through the loop.

- Changes to a resource's spec (in other words, its configuration values) trigger the reconcile loop. Therefore, it is often not enough to simply check for the existence of expected child resources. The Operator also needs to verify that the child resource configuration matches what is defined in the parent resource at the time of reconciliation.

- Reconciliation is not necessarily called for each change to the resource. It is possible that a single reconciliation may contain multiple changes. The Operator must be careful to ensure the entire state of the CR is represented by all of its child resources.

- Just because an Operator does not need to make changes during a reconciliation request doesn't mean it doesn't need to update the CR's Status field. Depending on what values are captured in the CR's status, it may make sense to update these even if the Operator determines it doesn't need to make any changes to the existing resources.

Operator Impact

It is important to be aware of the impact your Operator will have on the cluster. In most cases, your Operator will create one or more resources. It also needs to communicate with the cluster through the Kubernetes APIs. If the Operator incorrectly handles these operations, they can negatively affect the performance of the entire cluster.

How best to handle this varies from Operator to Operator. There is no set of rules that you can run through to ensure your Operator doesn't overburden your cluster. However, you can use the following guidelines as a starting point to analyze your Operator's approach:

- Be careful when making frequent calls to the Kubernetes API. Make sure you use sensible delays (on the order of seconds rather than milliseconds) when repeatedly checking the API for a certain state being met.

- When possible, try not to block the reconcile method for long periods of time. If, for instance, you are waiting for a child resource to be available before continuing, consider triggering another reconcile after a delay (see "The Reconcile Function" on page 69 for more information on triggering subsequent iterations through the reconcile loop). This approach allows Kubernetes to manage its resources instead of having a reconcile request wait for long periods of time.

- If you are deploying a large number of resources, consider throttling the deployment requests across multiple iterations through the reconcile loop. Remember that other workloads are running concurrently on the cluster. Your Operator should not cause excessive stress on cluster resources by issuing many creation requests at once.

Running an Operator Locally

The Operator SDK provides a means of running an Operator outside of a running cluster. This helps speed up development and testing by removing the need to go through the image creation and hosting steps. The process running the Operator may be outside of the cluster, but Kubernetes will treat it as it does any other controller.

The high-level steps for testing an Operator are as follows:

1. *Deploy the CRD.* You only need to do this once, unless further changes to the CRD are needed. In those cases, run the `kubectl apply` command again (from the Operator project root directory) to apply any changes:

   ```
   $ kubectl apply -f deploy/crds/*_crd.yaml
   ```

2. *Start the Operator in local mode.* The Operator SDK uses credentials from the `kubectl` configuration file to connect to the cluster and attach the Operator. The running process acts as if it were an Operator pod running inside of the cluster and writes logging information to standard output:

   ```
   $ export OPERATOR_NAME=<operator-name>
   $ operator-sdk up local --namespace default
   ```

   The `--namespace` flag indicates the namespace in which the Operator will appear to be running.

3. *Deploy an example resource.* The SDK generates an example CR along with the CRD. It is located in the same directory and is named similarly to the CRD, but with the filename ending in *_cr.yaml* instead to denote its function.

   In most cases, you'll want to edit the `spec` section of this file to provide the relevant configuration values for your resource. Once the necessary changes are made, deploy the CR (from the project root directory) using `kubectl`:

   ```
   $ kubectl apply -f deploy/crds/*_cr.yaml
   ```

4. *Stop the running Operator process.* Stop the Operator process by pressing Ctrl+C. Unless the Operator adds finalizers to the CR, this is safe to do before deleting the CR itself, as Kubernetes will use the parent/child relationships of its resources to clean up any dependent objects.

 The process described here is useful for development purposes, but for production, Operators are delivered as images. See Appendix A for more information on how to build and deploy an Operator as a container inside the cluster.

Visitors Site Example

The codebase for the Visitors Site Operator is too large to include. You can find the fully built Operator available in this book's GitHub repository (*https://github.com/ kubernetes-operators-book/chapters/tree/master/ch07/visitors-operator*).

The Operator SDK generated many of the files in that repository. The files that were modified to run the Visitors Site application are:

deploy/crds/
- *example_v1_visitorsapp_crd.yaml*
  — This file contains the CRD.
- *example_v1_visitorsapp_cr.yaml*
  — This file defines a CR with sensible example data.

pkg/apis/example/v1/visitorsapp_types.go
- This file contains Go objects that represent the CR, including its spec and status fields.

pkg/controller/visitorsapp/
- *backend.go, frontend.go, mysql.go*
  — These files contain all of the information specific to deploying those components of the Visitors Site. This includes the deployments and services that the Operator maintains, as well as the logic to handle updating existing resources when the end user changes the CR.
- *common.go*
  — This file contains utility methods used to ensure the deployments and services are running, creating them if necessary.

- *visitorsapp_controller.go*
  - The Operator SDK initially generated this file, which was then modified for the Visitors Site–specific logic. The `Reconcile` method contains the majority of the changes; it drives the overall flow of the Operator by calling out to functions in the previously described files.

Summary

Writing an Operator requires a considerable amount of code to tie into Kubernetes as a controller. The Operator SDK eases development by generating much of this boilerplate code, letting you focus on the business logic aspects. The SDK also provides utilities for building and testing Operators, greatly reducing the effort needed to go from inception to a running Operator.

Resources

- Kubernetes CR documentation (*https://oreil.ly/IwYGV*)
- Kubernetes API documentation (*https://godoc.org/k8s.io/api*)

CHAPTER 8

Operator Lifecycle Manager

Once you have written an Operator, it's time to turn your attention to its installation and management. As there are multiple steps involved in deploying an Operator, including creating the deployment, adding the custom resource definitions, and configuring the necessary permissions, a management layer becomes necessary to facilitate the process.

Operator Lifecycle Manager (OLM) fulfills this role by introducing a packaging mechanism for delivering Operators and the necessary metadata for visualizing them in compatible UIs, including installation instructions and API hints in the form of CRD descriptors.

OLM's benefits extend beyond installation into Day 2 operations, including managing upgrades to existing Operators, providing a means to convey Operator stability through version channels, and the ability to aggregate multiple Operator hosting sources into a single interface.

We begin this chapter by introducing OLM and its interfaces, including both the CRDs that end users will interact with inside of the cluster and the packaging format it uses for Operators. After that, we will show you OLM in action, using it to connect to OperatorHub.io to install an Operator. We conclude the chapter with a developer-focused exploration of the process of writing the necessary metadata files to make an Operator available to OLM and test it against a local cluster.

OLM Custom Resources

As you know, the CRDs owned by an Operator make up that Operator's API. So, it makes sense to look at each of the CRDs that are installed by OLM and explore their uses.

ClusterServiceVersion

The *ClusterServiceVersion* (CSV) is the primary metadata resource that describes an Operator. Each CSV represents a version of an Operator and contains the following:

- General metadata about the Operator, including its name, version, description, and icon
- Operator installation information, describing the deployments that are created and the permissions that are required
- The CRDs that are owned by the Operator as well as references to any CRDs the Operator is dependent on
- Annotations on the CRD fields to provide hints to users on how to properly specify values for the fields

When learning about CSVs, it can be useful to relate the concepts to that of a traditional Linux system. You can think of a CSV as analogous to a Linux package, such as a Red Hat Package Manager (RPM) file. Like an RPM file, the CSV contains information on how to install the Operator and any dependencies it requires. Following this analogy, you can think of OLM as a management tool similar to yum or DNF.

Another important aspect to understand is the relationship between a CSV and the Operator deployment resource it manages. Much like how a deployment describes the "pod template" for the pods it creates, a CSV contains a "deployment template" for the deployment of the Operator pod. This is a formal ownership in the Kubernetes sense of the word; if the Operator deployment is deleted, the CSV will recreate it to bring the cluster back to the desired state, similar to how a deployment will cause deleted pods to be recreated.

A ClusterServiceVersion resource is typically populated from a Cluster Service Version YAML file. We provide more details on how to write this file in "Writing a Cluster Service Version File" on page 93.

CatalogSource

A *CatalogSource* contains information for accessing a repository of Operators. OLM provides a utility API named `packagemanifests` for querying catalog sources, which provides a list of Operators and the catalogs in which they are found. It uses resources of this kind to populate the list of available Operators. The following is an example of using the `packagemanifests` API against the default catalog source:

```
$ kubectl -n olm get packagemanifests
NAME                          CATALOG               AGE
akka-cluster-operator         Community Operators   19s
appsody-operator              Community Operators   19s
[...]
```

Subscription

End users create a *subscription* to install, and subsequently update, the Operators that OLM provides. A subscription is made to a *channel*, which is a stream of Operator versions, such as "stable" or "nightly."

To continue with the earlier analogy to Linux packages, a subscription is equivalent to a command that installs a package, such as yum install. An installation command through yum will typically refer to the package by name rather than to a specific version, leaving the determination of the latest package to yum itself. In the same way, a subscription to an Operator by name and its channel lets OLM resolve the version based on what is available in that particular channel.

Users configure a subscription with an *approval mode*. This value, set to either manual or automatic, tells OLM if manual user review is required before an Operator is installed. If set to manual approval, OLM-compatible user interfaces present the user with the details of the resources OLM will create during the Operator installation. The user has the option of approving or rejecting the Operator, and OLM takes the appropriate next steps.

InstallPlan

A subscription creates an *InstallPlan*, which describes the full list of resources that OLM will create to satisfy the CSV's resource requirements. For subscriptions set to require manual approval, the end user sets an approval on this resource to inform OLM that the installation should proceed. Otherwise, users do not need to explicitly interact with these resources.

OperatorGroup

End users control Operator multitenancy through an *OperatorGroup*. These designate namespaces that may be accessed by an individual Operator. In other words, an Operator belonging to an OperatorGroup will not react to custom resource changes in a namespace not indicated by the group.

Although you can use OperatorGroups for fine-grained control for a set of namespaces, they are most commonly used in two ways:

- To scope an Operator to a single namespace
- To allow an Operator to run globally across all namespaces

For example, the following definition creates a group that scopes Operators within it to the single namespace ns-alpha:

```
apiVersion: operators.coreos.com/v1alpha2
kind: OperatorGroup
metadata:
  name: group-alpha
  namespace: ns-alpha
spec:
  targetNamespaces:
  - ns-alpha
```

Omitting the designator entirely results in a group that will cover all namespaces in the cluster:

```
apiVersion: operators.coreos.com/v1alpha2
kind: OperatorGroup
metadata:
  name: group-alpha
  namespace: ns-alpha ❶
```

❶ Note that, as a Kubernetes resource, the OperatorGroup must still reside in a specific namespace. However, the lack of the `targetNamespaces` designation means the OperatorGroup will cover all namespaces.

> The two examples shown here cover the majority of use cases; creating fine-grained OperatorGroups scoped to more than one specific namespace is outside the scope of this book. You can find more information in OLM's GitHub repository (*https://oreil.ly/ZBAou*).

Installing OLM

In the rest of this chapter, we explore using and developing for OLM. As OLM is not installed by default in most Kubernetes distributions, the first step is to install the necessary resources to run it.

> OLM is an evolving project. As such, be sure to consult its GitHub repository to find the latest installation instructions for the current release (*https://oreil.ly/It369*). You can find the most recent releases on the OLM project's GitHub repository.

As of the current release (0.11.0), the installation performs two primary tasks.

To begin, you'll need to install the CRDs required by OLM. These function as the API into OLM and provide the ability to configure external sources that provide Operators and the cluster-side resources used to make those Operators available to users. You create these through the `kubectl apply` command, as follows:

```
$ kubectl apply -f \
https://github.com/operator-framework/operator-lifecycle-manager/releases/\
download/0.11.0/crds.yaml
clusterserviceversions.operators.coreos.com created
installplans.operators.coreos.com created
subscriptions.operators.coreos.com created
catalogsources.operators.coreos.com created
operatorgroups.operators.coreos.com created
```

> The examples here use the 0.11.0 release, which was the latest version at the time of writing; you can update these commands to use the most up-to-date version available at the time you're reading the book.

The second step is to create all of the Kubernetes resources that make up OLM itself. These include the Operators that will drive OLM as well as the necessary RBAC resources (ServiceAccounts, ClusterRoles, etc.) for it to function.

As with the CRD creation, you perform this step through the kubectl apply command:

```
$ kubectl apply -f \
https://github.com/operator-framework/operator-lifecycle-manager/\
releases/download/0.11.0/olm.yaml
namespace/olm created
namespace/operators created
system:controller:operator-lifecycle-manager created
serviceaccount/olm-operator-serviceaccount created
clusterrolebinding.rbac.authorization.k8s.io/olm-operator-binding-olm created
deployment.apps/olm-operator created
deployment.apps/catalog-operator created
clusterrole.rbac.authorization.k8s.io/aggregate-olm-edit created
clusterrole.rbac.authorization.k8s.io/aggregate-olm-view created
operatorgroup.operators.coreos.com/global-operators created
operatorgroup.operators.coreos.com/olm-operators created
clusterserviceversion.operators.coreos.com/packageserver created
catalogsource.operators.coreos.com/operatorhubio-catalog created
```

You can verify the installation by looking at the resources that were created:

```
$ kubectl get ns olm
NAME            STATUS    AGE
olm             Active    43s


$ kubectl get pods -n olm
NAME                             READY   STATUS    RESTARTS   AGE
catalog-operator-7c94984c6c-wpxsv   1/1     Running   0          68s
olm-operator-79fdbcc897-r76ss    1/1     Running   0          68s
olm-operators-qlkh2              1/1     Running   0          57s
operatorhubio-catalog-9jdd8      1/1     Running   0          57s
packageserver-654686f57d-74skk   1/1     Running   0          39s
```

```
packageserver-654686f57d-b8ckz     1/1     Running   0          39s
```

```
$ kubectl get crd
NAME                                           CREATED AT
catalogsources.operators.coreos.com            2019-08-07T20:30:42Z
clusterserviceversions.operators.coreos.com    2019-08-07T20:30:42Z
installplans.operators.coreos.com              2019-08-07T20:30:42Z
operatorgroups.operators.coreos.com            2019-08-07T20:30:42Z
subscriptions.operators.coreos.com             2019-08-07T20:30:42Z
```

Using OLM

Now that we've introduced the basic concepts around OLM, let's see how to use it to install an Operator. We'll use OperatorHub.io as the source repository for Operators. We cover OperatorHub.io in more detail in Chapter 10, but for now the important thing to know is that it's a community-curated list of publicly available Operators for use with OLM. In keeping with the Linux package analogy from earlier in the chapter, you can think of it as similar to an RPM repository.

Installing OLM creates a default catalog source in the olm namespace. You can verify that this source, named operatorhubio-catalog, exists by using the CLI:

```
$ kubectl get catalogsource -n olm
NAME                  NAME                 TYPE   PUBLISHER      AGE
operatorhubio-catalog Community Operators  grpc   OperatorHub.io 4h20m
```

You can find further details about the source by using the describe command:

```
$ kubectl describe catalogsource/operatorhubio-catalog -n olm
Name:         operatorhubio-catalog
Namespace:    olm
Labels:       <none>
Annotations:  kubectl.kubernetes.io/last-applied-configuration...
API Version:  operators.coreos.com/v1alpha1
Kind:         CatalogSource
Metadata:
  Creation Timestamp:  2019-09-23T13:53:39Z
  Generation:          1
  Resource Version:    801
  Self Link:           /apis/operators.coreos.com/v1alpha1/...
  UID:                 45842de1-3b6d-4b1b-bd36-f616dec94c6a
Spec:
  Display Name:  Community Operators  ❶
  Image:         quay.io/operator-framework/upstream-community-operators:latest
  Publisher:     OperatorHub.io
  Source Type:   grpc
Status:
  Last Sync:  2019-09-23T13:53:54Z
  Registry Service:
    Created At:         2019-09-23T13:53:44Z
    Port:               50051
```

```
    Protocol:            grpc
    Service Name:        operatorhubio-catalog
    Service Namespace:   olm
  Events:                <none>
```

❶ Note that the display name is simply "Community Operators," rather than indicating anything about OperatorHub.io. This value appears in the output of the
next command, when we look at the list of possible Operators.

This catalog source is configured to read all of the Operators hosted on
OperatorHub.io. You can use the `packagemanifest` utility API to get a list of the
Operators that are found:

```
$ kubectl get packagemanifest -n olm
NAME                         CATALOG               AGE
akka-cluster-operator        Community Operators   4h47m
appsody-operator             Community Operators   4h47m
aqua                         Community Operators   4h47m
atlasmap-operator            Community Operators   4h47m
[...] ❶
```

❶ At the time of writing, there are close to 80 Operators on OperatorHub.io. We
truncated the output of this command for brevity.

For this example, you'll install the etcd Operator. The first step is to define an OperatorGroup to dictate which namespaces the Operator will manage. The etcd Operator
you're going to be using is scoped to a single namespace (you'll see later how we
determined that), so you'll create a group for just the default namespace:

```
apiVersion: operators.coreos.com/v1alpha2
kind: OperatorGroup
metadata:
  name: default-og
  namespace: default
spec:
  targetNamespaces:
  - default
```

Create the group using the `kubectl apply` command (this example assumes the
YAML in the previous snippet is saved to a file named *all-og.yaml*):

```
$ kubectl apply -f all-og.yaml
operatorgroup.operators.coreos.com/default-og created
```

The creation of a subscription triggers the installation of an Operator. Before you can
do that, you need to determine which channel you want to subscribe to. OLM provides channel information in addition to a wealth of other details about the Operator.

You can view this information by using the `packagemanifest` API:

```
$ kubectl describe packagemanifest/etcd -n olm
Name:          etcd
Namespace:     olm
Labels:        catalog=operatorhubio-catalog
               catalog-namespace=olm
               provider=CNCF
               provider-url=
Annotations:   <none>
API Version:   packages.operators.coreos.com/v1
Kind:          PackageManifest
Metadata:
  Creation Timestamp:  2019-09-23T13:53:39Z
  Self Link:           /apis/packages.operators.coreos.com/v1/namespaces/...
Spec:
Status:
  Catalog Source:                operatorhubio-catalog
  Catalog Source Display Name:   Community Operators
  Catalog Source Namespace:      olm
  Catalog Source Publisher:      OperatorHub.io
  Channels:
    Current CSV:  etcdoperator.v0.9.4-clusterwide
    Current CSV Desc:
      Annotations:
        Alm - Examples:  [...]   ❶
[...]  ❷
      Install Modes:  ❸
          Type:        OwnNamespace
          Supported:   true   ❹
          Type:        SingleNamespace
          Supported:   true
          Type:        MultiNamespace
          Supported:   false
          Type:        AllNamespaces
          Supported:   false   ❺
      Provider:
          Name:      CNCF
      Version:       0.9.4
  Name:          singlenamespace-alpha   ❻
    Default Channel:  singlenamespace-alpha
    Package Name:     etcd
    Provider:
      Name:  CNCF
[...]
```

❶ The examples section of a package manifest contains a series of manifests that you can use to deploy custom resources defined by this Operator. For brevity, we have omitted them from this output.

❷ We cut out much of the file for readability. We'll cover many of these fields when we talk about creating the CSV file in "Writing a Cluster Service Version File" on page 93.

❸ The install modes section describes the circumstances in which an end user may deploy this Operator. We will also cover these later in this chapter.

❹ This particular channel offers an Operator that is configured to be run to watch the same namespace it is deployed in.

❺ Along the same lines, end users cannot install this Operator to monitor all namespaces in the cluster. If you look around in the package manifest data you'll find another channel named `clusterwide-alpha` that is suited to this purpose.

❻ The `Name` field in this section indicates the name of the channel which is referenced by a subscription.

Since this Operator comes from OperatorHub.io, it can be beneficial to view its page on the site directly. All of the data contained in the package manifest is displayed on the individual Operator's page, but formatted in a more easily readable manner. You can check this out on the etcd Operator page (*https://oreil.ly/1bjkr*).

Once you have decided on a channel, the last step is to create the subscription resource itself. Here is an example manifest:

```
apiVersion: operators.coreos.com/v1alpha1
kind: Subscription
metadata:
  name: etcd-subscription
  namespace: default ❶
spec:
  name: etcd ❷
  source: operatorhubio-catalog ❸
  sourceNamespace: olm
  channel: singlenamespace-alpha ❹
```

❶ This manifest installs the subscription, and thus the Operator deployment itself, in the default namespace.

❷ The name of the Operator to be installed, as found by the `packagemanifest` API call.

❸ The `source` and `sourceNamespace` describe where to find the catalog source that provides the Operator.

❹ OLM will install Operators from the `singlenamespace-alpha` channel.

As with other resources, you create the subscription using `kubectl apply` (this command assumes the subscription YAML above is saved in a file named *sub.yaml*):

```
$ kubectl apply -f sub.yaml
subscription.operators.coreos.com/etcd-subscription created
```

Exploring the Operator

When you create the subscription, a number of things happen. At the highest level of the resource hierarchy, OLM creates a ClusterServiceVersion resource in the default namespace:

```
$ kubectl get csv -n default
NAME                     DISPLAY   VERSION   REPLACES               PHASE
etcdoperator.v0.9.4      etcd      0.9.4     etcdoperator.v0.9.2    Succeeded
```

The CSV is effectively what the subscription installs—it's the package, in the RPM analogy. OLM performs the Operator installation steps defined in the CSV to create the Operator pods themselves. Additionally, OLM will store information about events in this process, which you can view using the describe command:

```
$ kubectl describe csv/etcdoperator.v0.9.4 -n default
[...]
Events:
operator-lifecycle-manager  requirements not yet checked
one or more requirements couldn't be found
all requirements found, attempting install
waiting for install components to report healthy
installing: ComponentMissing: missing deployment with name=etcd-operator
installing: ComponentMissing: missing deployment with name=etcd-operator
installing: Waiting: waiting for deployment etcd-operator to become ready:
   Waiting for rollout to finish: 0 of 1 updated replicas are available...
install strategy completed with no errors
```

 The output here has been edited to fit the page. Your output will vary slightly and contain more data per event.

OLM is responsible for following the deployment template contained within the CSV to create the Operator pod itself. Continuing down the resource ownership hierarchy, you can see that OLM creates a deployment resource as well:

```
$ kubectl get deployment -n default
NAME            READY   UP-TO-DATE   AVAILABLE   AGE
etcd-operator   1/1     1            1           3m42s
```

Viewing the details of the deployment explicitly shows the owner relationship between the CSV and this deployment:

```
$ kubectl get deployment/etcd-operator -n default -o yaml
[...]
ownerReferences:
```

```
- apiVersion: operators.coreos.com/v1alpha1
  blockOwnerDeletion: false
  controller: false
  kind: ClusterServiceVersion
  name: etcdoperator.v0.9.4
  uid: 564c15d9-ab49-439f-8ea4-8c140f55e641
[...]
```

Unsurprisingly, the deployment creates a number of pods based on its resource definition. In the case of the etcd Operator, the CSV defines the deployment as requiring three pods:

```
$ kubectl get pods -n default
NAME                             READY   STATUS    RESTARTS   AGE
etcd-operator-c4bc4fb66-zg22g    3/3     Running   0          6m4s
```

To summarize, creating the subscription caused the following to take place:

- OLM creates a CSV resource in the same namespace as the subscription. This CSV contains, among other things, the manifest for the deployment of the Operator itself.

- OLM uses the deployment manifest to create a deployment resource for the Operator. The owner of that resource is the CSV itself.

- The deployment causes the creation of replica sets and pods for the Operator itself.

Deleting the Operator

Deleting an OLM-deployed Operator isn't as straightforward as it is when working with simple deployment resources.

A deployment resource acts as installation instructions for pods. If a pod is removed, either by user intervention or because of an error on the pod itself, Kubernetes detects the difference between the desired state of the deployment and the actual number of pods.

In much the same way, the CSV resource acts as the installation instructions for the Operator. Often, a CSV indicates that a deployment must exist to fulfill this plan. If that deployment ceases to exist, OLM takes the necessary steps to make the actual state of the system match the CSV's desired state.

As such, it's not sufficient to simply delete the Operator's deployment resource. Instead, an Operator deployed by OLM is deleted by deleting the CSV resource:

```
$ kubectl delete csv/etcdoperator.v0.9.4
clusterserviceversion.operators.coreos.com "etcdoperator.v0.9.4" deleted
```

OLM takes care of deleting the resources that the CSV created when it was originally deployed, including the Operator's deployment resource.

Additionally, you'll need to delete the subscription to prevent OLM from installing new CSV versions in the future:

```
$ kubectl delete subscription/etcd-subscription
subscription.operators.coreos.com "etcd-subscription" deleted
```

OLM Bundle Metadata Files

An "OLM bundle" provides details on an Operator that can be installed. The bundle contains all the necessary information (for all the available versions of the Operator) to:

- Provide a flexible delivery structure for the Operator by offering one or more *channels* that a user can subscribe to.
- Deploy the CRDs required for the Operator to function.
- Instruct OLM on how to create the Operator deployment.
- Include additional information on each CRD spec field, including hints on how to render those fields in a UI.

There are three types of files included in an OLM bundle: custom resource definitions, Cluster Service Version files, and package manifest files.

Custom Resource Definitions

Since the Operator requires its CRDs to function, the OLM bundle includes them. OLM installs the CRDs along with the Operator itself. You, as the OLM bundle developer, do not need to make any changes or additions to the CRD files beyond what already exists to support the Operator.

Keep in mind that only CRDs that are owned by the Operator should be included. Any dependent CRDs that are provided by other Operators will be installed automatically by OLM's dependency resolution (the notion of required CRDs is addressed in "Owned CRDs" on page 96).

 Each CRD must be defined in its own file.

Cluster Service Version File

The CSV file contains the bulk of the metadata about the Operator, including:

- How to deploy the Operator
- The list of CRDs that the Operator uses (those that it owns as well as dependencies from other Operators)
- Metadata about the Operator, including a description, logo, its maturity level, and related links

Given the large role this file plays, we cover details on how to write one in the following section.

Package Manifest File

The package manifest file describes a list of channels that point to particular Operator versions. It is up to the Operator owners to determine the breakdown of channels and their respective delivery cadence. We strongly recommend that channels set expectations around stability, features, and rate of changes.

Users subscribe to channels. OLM will use the package manifest to determine if a new version of the Operator is available in a subscribed-to channel and allow the user to take steps to update as appropriate. We'll get into more detail about this file in "Writing a Package Manifest File" on page 101.

Writing a Cluster Service Version File

Each version of an Operator will have its own Cluster Service Version file. The CSV file is a standard Kubernetes manifest of kind ClusterServiceVersion, which is one of the custom resources that OLM provides.

The resources in this file provide OLM with information about a specific Operator version, including installation instructions and extra details on how the user interacts with the Operator's CRDs.

Generating a File Skeleton

Given the amount of data included in a CSV file, the easiest starting point is to use the Operator SDK to generate a skeleton. The SDK will build this skeleton with the basic structure of a Cluster Service Version file, and will populate it with as much data as it can determine about the Operator itself. It provides a good basis from which you can flesh out the remaining details.

As each CSV corresponds to a particular Operator version, that version information is reflected in the filename scheme. The filename pattern is to use the Operator name and append the semantic version number. For example, a CSV file for the Visitors Site Operator will be named something like *visitors-operator.v1.0.0.yaml*.

In order for the Operator SDK to populate the skeleton CSV file with information about a specific Operator, you must run the generation command from the root of the Operator project source code. The general form of this command is as follows:

```
$ operator-sdk olm-catalog gen-csv --csv-version x.y.z
```

Again, is it up to the Operator's development team to determine their own version numbering policy. For consistency and general user-friendliness, we recommend that Operator releases follow Semantic Versioning (*https://semver.org*) principles.

Running the CSV generation command on the Visitors Site Operator produces the following output:

```
$ operator-sdk olm-catalog gen-csv --csv-version 1.0.0
INFO[0000] Generating CSV manifest version 1.0.0
INFO[0000] Fill in the following required fields in file
visitors-operator/1.0.0/visitors-operator.v1.0.0.clusterserviceversion.yaml:
    spec.keywords
    spec.maintainers
    spec.provider
INFO[0000] Created
visitors-operator/1.0.0/visitors-operator.v1.0.0.clusterserviceversion.yaml
```

Even with only the base CSV structure, the generated file is already fairly detailed. At a high level, it includes the following:

- References to all CRDs the Operator owns (in other words, those defined in the Operator project)
- A partial definition for the Operator's Deployment resource
- A set of RBAC rules that the Operator requires
- Indicators describing the scope of namespaces the Operator will watch
- An example custom resource (found in `metadata.annotations.alm-examples`) that you can modify for your needs

We dive deeper into each of these components and the sorts of changes you should make to them in the following sections.

The SDK will not know the name of the image to use for the Operator itself. The skeleton file includes the field `image: REPLACE_IMAGE` in the deployment descriptor. You must update this value to point to a hosted image of the Operator (for example, on Docker Hub or Quay.io) that OLM will deploy.

Metadata

As previously mentioned, the `metadata.annotations.alm-examples` field contains an example for each CRD that the Operator owns. The SDK will initially populate this field using the custom resource manifest found in the Operator project's *deploy/crds* directory. Be sure to review and flesh out this example with actual data that end users can further customize to their needs.

Apart from `alm-examples`, you can find the remainder of the Operator's metadata under the `spec` section of the manifest. The output of the SDK's generation command highlights three specific fields as required:

keywords
> A list of categories describing the Operator; compatible UIs use this for discovery

maintainers
> A list of name and email pairings for the maintainers of the Operator codebase

provider
> The name of the publishing entity for the Operator

This snippet from the etcd Operator demonstrates the three required fields:

```
keywords: ['etcd', 'key value', 'database', 'coreos', 'open source']
maintainers:
- name: etcd Community
  email: etcd-dev@googlegroups.com
provider:
  name: CNCF
```

We also encourage you to provide the following metadata fields, which produce a more robust listing in catalogs such as OperatorHub.io:

displayName
> A user-friendly name for the Operator

description
> A string describing the Operator's functionality; you can use YAML constructs for multiline strings to provide further display information

version
> The semantic version of the Operator, which should be incremented each time a new Operator image is published

replaces
> The version, if any, of the Operator that this CSV updates

icon
> A base64–encoded image used by compatible UIs

maturity
> The maturity level of the Operator included in this release, such as alpha, beta, or stable

links
> A list of relevant links for the Operator, such as documentation, quick start guides, or blog entries

minKubeVersion
> The minimum version of Kubernetes that the Operator must be deployed on, using the format "Major.Minor.Patch" (e.g., 1.13.0)

Owned CRDs

In order to install an Operator, OLM must know about all of the CRDs it uses. These come in two forms: those owned by the Operator and those that are used as dependencies (in CSV terms, these are referred to as "required" CRDs; we will cover these in the next section).

The SDK skeleton generation adds the spec.customresourcedefinitions section to the CSV file. It also populates the owned section with entries for each CRD defined by the Operator, including identifying information such as kind, name, and version. However, there are more fields that you must manually add before the OLM bundle is valid.

The following are required fields that you must set for each owned CRD:

displayName
> The user-friendly name of the custom resource

description
> Information about what the custom resource represents

resources
> A list of Kubernetes resource types that will be created by the custom resource

The resources list does not need to be exhaustive. Rather, it should only list visible resources that are relevant to the user. For example, you should list things an end user interacts with, such as service and deployment resources, but omit an internal ConfigMap that the user does not directly manipulate.

You only need to include one instance of each resource type, regardless of how many resources of that type are created by the Operator. For example, if the custom resource creates multiple deployments, you only need to list the deployment resource type once.

An example list for a custom resource that creates one or more deployments and services is as follows:

```
resources:
- kind: Service
  version: v1
- kind: Deployment
  version: v1
```

There are two more fields you need to add to each owned resource: `specDescriptors` and `statusDescriptors`. These fields provide additional metadata about the `spec` and `status` fields that will be present in the custom resource. Compatible UIs can use this additional information to render an interface for users.

For each field in the custom resource's spec, add an entry to the `specDescriptors` field. Each entry should contain the following:

displayName
> The user-friendly name of the field

description
> Information about what the field represents

path
> The dot-delimited path of the field in the object

x-descriptors
> UI component information about the field's capabilities

Table 8-1 lists the descriptors that are commonly supported by compatible UIs.

Table 8-1. Commonly used spec descriptors

Type	Descriptor string
Boolean switch	`urn:alm:descriptor:com.tectonic.ui:booleanSwitch`
Checkbox	`urn:alm:descriptor:com.tectonic.ui:checkbox`
Endpoint list	`urn:alm:descriptor:com.tectonic.ui:endpointList`
Image pull policy	`urn:alm:descriptor:com.tectonic.ui:imagePullPolicy`
Label	`urn:alm:descriptor:com.tectonic.ui:label`
Namespace selector	`urn:alm:descriptor:com.tectonic.ui:namespaceSelector`
Node affinity	`urn:alm:descriptor:com.tectonic.ui:nodeAffinity`
Number	`urn:alm:descriptor:com.tectonic.ui:number`
Password	`urn:alm:descriptor:com.tectonic.ui:password`
Pod affinity	`urn:alm:descriptor:com.tectonic.ui:podAffinity`
Pod anti-affinity	`urn:alm:descriptor:com.tectonic.ui:podAntiAffinity`
Resource requirements	`urn:alm:descriptor:com.tectonic.ui:resourceRequirements`

Type	Descriptor string
Selector	`urn:alm:descriptor:com.tectonic.ui:selector:`
Text	`urn:alm:descriptor:com.tectonic.ui:text`
Update strategy	`urn:alm:descriptor:com.tectonic.ui:updateStrategy`

The structure of the `statusDescriptors` field is similar, including the same fields you need to specify. The only difference is the set of valid descriptors; these are listed in Table 8-2.

Table 8-2. Commonly used status descriptors

Type	Descriptor string
Conditions	`urn:alm:descriptor:io.kubernetes.conditions`
k8s phase reason	`urn:alm:descriptor:io.kubernetes.phase:reason`
k8s phase	`urn:alm:descriptor:io.kubernetes.phase`
Pod count	`urn:alm:descriptor:com.tectonic.ui:podCount`
Pod statuses	`urn:alm:descriptor:com.tectonic.ui:podStatuses`
Prometheus endpoint	`urn:alm:descriptor:prometheusEndpoint`
Text	`urn:alm:descriptor:text`
W3 link	`urn:alm:descriptor:org.w3:link`

As an example, the following snippet contains a subset of the descriptors for the etcd Operator:

```
specDescriptors:
- description: The desired number of member Pods for the etcd cluster.
    displayName: Size
    path: size
    x-descriptors:
    - 'urn:alm:descriptor:com.tectonic.ui:podCount'
- description: Limits describes the minimum/maximum amount of compute
                resources required/allowed
    displayName: Resource Requirements
    path: pod.resources
    x-descriptors:
    - 'urn:alm:descriptor:com.tectonic.ui:resourceRequirements'

statusDescriptors:
- description: The status of each of the member Pods for the etcd cluster.
    displayName: Member Status
    path: members
    x-descriptors:
    - 'urn:alm:descriptor:com.tectonic.ui:podStatuses'
- description: The current size of the etcd cluster.
    displayName: Cluster Size
    path: size
```

```
    - description: The current status of the etcd cluster.
      displayName: Status
      path: phase
      x-descriptors:
      - 'urn:alm:descriptor:io.kubernetes.phase'
    - description: Explanation for the current status of the cluster.
      displayName: Status Details
      path: reason
      x-descriptors:
      - 'urn:alm:descriptor:io.kubernetes.phase:reason'
```

Required CRDs

Custom resources that are used by an Operator but not owned by it are designated as *required*. When installing an Operator, OLM will find the appropriate Operator that provides a required CRD and install it. This allows Operators to maintain a limited scope while utilizing composition and dependency resolution when necessary.

The required section of a CSV is optional. Only Operators that require the use of other, non-Kubernetes resources need to include this.

Each required CRD is specified using its:

name
> The full name used to identify the required CRD

version
> The version of the CRD desired

kind
> The Kubernetes resource kind; displayed to users in compatible UIs

displayName
> The user-friendly name of the field; displayed to users in compatible UIs

description
> Information on how the required CRD is used; displayed to users in compatible UIs

For example, the following indicates an EtcdCluster is a required CRD for a different Operator:

```
required:
- name: etcdclusters.etcd.database.coreos.com
  version: v1beta2
  kind: EtcdCluster
  displayName: etcd Cluster
  description: Represents a cluster of etcd nodes.
```

One entry is needed under the required field for each required CRD.

Install Modes

The install modes section of a CSV tells OLM how the Operator can be deployed. There are four options, all of which must be present in the `installModes` field with their own flag indicating whether or not they are supported. The Operator SDK includes a default set of values for each of these options when generating a CSV.

The following installation modes are supported:

OwnNamespace
> The Operator can be deployed to an OperatorGroup that selects its own namespace.

SingleNamespace
> The Operator can be deployed to an OperatorGroup that selects one namespace.

MultiNamespace
> The Operator can be deployed to an OperatorGroup that selects more than one namespace.

AllNamespaces
> The Operator can be deployed to an OperatorGroup that selects all namespaces (defined as `targetNamespace: ""`).

The following snippet shows the proper way to structure this field, along with the default values set by the SDK during generation:

```
installModes:
- type: OwnNamespace
  supported: true
- type: SingleNamespace
  supported: true
- type: MultiNamespace
  supported: false
- type: AllNamespaces
  supported: true
```

Versioning and Updating

True to its name, each Cluster Service Version file represents a single version of an Operator. Subsequent versions of the Operator will each have their own CSV file. In many cases, this can be a copy of the previous version with the appropriate changes.

The following describes the general changes you need to make between versions of an Operator (this is not an exhaustive list; take care to review the entire contents of the file to ensure no further changes are required):

- Change the new CSV filename to reflect the new version of the Operator.

- Update the `metadata.name` field of the CSV file with the new version.

- Update the `spec.version` field with the new version.

- Update the `spec.replaces` field to indicate the previous version of the CSV that is being upgraded by the new version.

- In most cases, the new CSV will refer to a newer image of the Operator itself. Be sure to update the `spec.containers.image` field as appropriate to refer to the correct image.

- In the event of a CRD change, you may need to update the `specDescriptor` and `statusDescriptor` fields of the CRD reference in the CSV file.

While these changes will result in a new version of the Operator, users cannot access that version until it is present in a channel. Update the *.package.yaml* file to reference the new CSV file for the appropriate channels (see the next section for more information on this file).

Do not modify existing CSV files once they are released and in use by OLM. Make changes in a new version of the file instead, and propagate it to users through the use of channels.

Writing a Package Manifest File

Compared to writing a Cluster Service Version file, writing a package manifest is significantly easier. A package file requires three fields:

packageName
: The name of the Operator itself; this should match the value used in the CSV file

channels
: A list of all channels for delivering versions of the Operator

defaultChannel
: The name of the channel users should subscribe to by default

Each entry in the `channels` field is made up of two items:

name
: The name of the channel; this is what users will subscribe to

currentCSV
: The full name (including the Operator name but not the *.yaml* suffix) of the CSV file that is currently installed through the channel

It is left to the Operator's team to determine their policy for what channels will be supported.

The following example distributes the Visitors Site Operator through two channels:

```
packageName: visitors-operator
channels:
- name: stable
  currentCSV: visitors-operator.v1.0.0
- name: testing
  currentCSV: visitors-operator.v1.1.0
defaultChannel: stable
```

Running Locally

Once you have written the necessary bundle files, the next step is to build the bundle and test it against a local cluster, such as one started by Minikube. In the following sections, we'll describe the process of installing OLM into a cluster, building the OLM bundle, and subscribing to a channel to deploy the Operator.

Prerequisites

This section covers the changes you need to make to the cluster to run OLM, as well as configuring it to look at your repository of bundles. You only need to complete these steps once for a cluster; we cover iterative development and testing of an Operator in "Building the OLM Bundle" on page 105.

Install the Marketplace Operator

The Marketplace Operator imports Operators from an external data store. In this chapter, you'll be using Quay.io to host your OLM bundles.

> Despite its name, the Marketplace Operator is not tied to a particular source of Operators. It simply acts as a conduit to pull Operators from any compatible external store. One such site is OperatorHub.io, which we discuss in Chapter 10.

In keeping with the notion that CRDs represent an Operator's API, installing the Marketplace Operator introduces two CRDs:

- The OperatorSource resource describes an external hosting registry for OLM bundles. In this example, we use Quay.io, a free image hosting site.

- The CatalogSourceConfig resource bridges between an OperatorSource and OLM itself. An OperatorSource automatically creates CatalogSourceConfig resources, and you do not need to explicitly interact with this type.

 Similar to OLM, the Marketplace Operator is an evolving project. As such, be sure to consult its GitHub repository (*https://oreil.ly/ VNOrU*) to find the latest installation instructions for the current release.

As there are currently no formal releases of the Marketplace Operator, it is installed by cloning the upstream repository and using the manifests within:

```
$ git clone https://github.com/operator-framework/operator-marketplace.git
$ cd operator-marketplace
$ kubectl apply -f deploy/upstream/
namespace/marketplace created
customresourcedefinition.apiextensions.k8s.io/catalogsourceconfigs.....
customresourcedefinition.apiextensions.k8s.io/operatorsources.operators....
serviceaccount/marketplace-operator created
clusterrole.rbac.authorization.k8s.io/marketplace-operator created
role.rbac.authorization.k8s.io/marketplace-operator created
clusterrolebinding.rbac.authorization.k8s.io/marketplace-operator created
rolebinding.rbac.authorization.k8s.io/marketplace-operator created
operatorsource.operators.coreos.com/upstream-community-operators created
deployment.apps/marketplace-operator created
```

You can verify the installation by ensuring the marketplace namespace was created:

```
$ kubectl get ns marketplace
NAME          STATUS   AGE
marketplace   Active   4m19s
```

Install Operator Courier

Operator Courier is a client-side tool used for building and pushing the OLM bundle to a repository. It is also used for verifying the contents of the bundle files.

You can install Operator Courier through the Python package installer pip:

```
$ pip3 install operator-courier
```

Once installed, you can run Operator Courier from the command line:

```
$ operator-courier
usage: operator-courier <command> [<args>]

These are the commands you can use:
    verify    Create a bundle and test it for correctness.
    push      Create a bundle, test it, and push it to an app registry.
    nest      Take a flat to-be-bundled directory and version nest it.
```

```
flatten      Create a flat directory from versioned operator bundle yaml
             files.
```

Retrieve a Quay token

Quay.io is a free hosting site for container images. We will use Quay.io to host the OLM bundles to serve them to the Operator Marketplace.

New users can sign up for a free Quay.io account via the website (*https://quay.io/*).

In order for Operator Courier to push OLM bundles into your Quay.io account, you need an authentication token. While the token is accessible through the web UI, you can also use the following script to retrieve it from the command line, substituting your username and password as indicated:

```
USERNAME=<quay.io username>
PASSWORD=<quay.io password>
URL=https://quay.io/cnr/api/v1/users/login

TOKEN_JSON=$(curl -s -H "Content-Type: application/json" -XPOST $URL -d \
'{"user":{"username":"'"${USERNAME}"'","password": "'"${PASSWORD}"'"}}')

echo `echo $TOKEN_JSON | awk '{split($0,a,"\""); print a[4]}'`
```

An interactive version of this script is provided in this book's GitHub repository (*https://github.com/kubernetes-operators-book/chapters/blob/master/ch08/get-quay-token*).

You will use this token later when pushing the bundle to Quay.io, so save it somewhere accessible. The output of the script provides a command to save it as an environment variable.

Create the OperatorSource

An OperatorSource resource defines the external data store used to host Operator bundles. In this case, you will be defining an OperatorSource to point to your Quay.io account, which will provide access to its hosted OLM bundles.

A sample OperatorSource manifest follows; you should replace both instances of <QUAY_USERNAME> with your Quay.io username:

```
apiVersion: operators.coreos.com/v1
kind: OperatorSource
metadata:
  name: <QUAY_USERNAME>-operators    ❶
  namespace: marketplace
spec:
  type: appregistry
  endpoint: https://quay.io/cnr
  registryNamespace: <QUAY_USERNAME>
```

❶ Using your username here isn't a hard requirement; it's just a simple way to ensure uniqueness for the OperatorSource name.

Once you've written the OperatorSource manifest, create the resource using the following command (assuming the manifest file is named *operator-source.yaml*):

```
$ kubectl apply -f operator-source.yaml
```

To verify the OperatorSource was deployed correctly, you can look in the market place namespace for a list of all known OperatorSources:

```
$ kubectl get opsrc -n marketplace
NAME             TYPE         ENDPOINT              REGISTRY  STATUS
jdob-operators   appregistry  https://quay.io/cnr  jdob      Failed ❶
```

❶ If there are no bundles at the endpoint when you create the source, the status will be Failed. You can ignore this for now; you'll refresh this list later, once you've uploaded a bundle.

The output shown here has been truncated for readability; your results may vary slightly.

When the OperatorSource is initially created, it may fail if there are no OLM bundles found in the user's Quay.io application list. In a later step, you will create and deploy the bundles, after which the OperatorSource will start correctly. We included this step as a prerequisite since you only need to do it once; when updating an OLM bundle or creating new ones in the same Quay.io namespace, you will reuse the OperatorSource resource.

Additionally, the OperatorSource creation results in the creation of a CatalogSource. No further action is required for this resource, but you can confirm its existence by checking in the marketplace namespace:

```
$ kubectl get catalogsource -n marketplace
NAME             NAME    TYPE  PUBLISHER  AGE
jdob-operators           grpc            6m5s
[...]
```

Building the OLM Bundle

Once you've installed the initial prerequisites, the bulk of your time is spent on a build and test cycle. This section covers the steps necessary to build and host an OLM bundle on Quay.io.

Perform linting

OLM bundles are verified using Operator Courier's `verify` command:

```
$ operator-courier verify $OLM_FILES_DIRECTORY
```

Push the bundle to Quay.io

When the metadata files pass verification and are ready to be tested, Operator Courier uploads the OLM bundle into your Quay.io account. There are a number of required parameters (and some optional arguments) when using the push command:

```
$ operator-courier push
usage: operator-courier [-h] [--validation-output VALIDATION_OUTPUT]
source_dir namespace repository release token
```

Here's an example push for the Visitors Site Operator:

```
OPERATOR_DIR=visitors-olm/
QUAY_NAMESPACE=jdob
PACKAGE_NAME=visitors-operator
PACKAGE_VERSION=1.0.0
QUAY_TOKEN=*****  ❶
$ operator-courier push "$OPERATOR_DIR" "$QUAY_NAMESPACE" \
"$PACKAGE_NAME" "$PACKAGE_VERSION" "$QUAY_TOKEN"
```

❶ QUAY_TOKEN is the full token, including the "basic" prefix. You can use the script we introduced earlier in this section to set this variable.

> By default, bundles pushed to Quay.io in this fashion are marked as private. Navigate to the image at *https://quay.io/application/* and mark it as public so that it is accessible to the cluster.

The Operator bundle is now ready for testing. For subsequent versions, update the `PACKAGE_VERSION` variable according to the new version of the CSV file (see "Versioning and Updating" on page 100 for more information) and push a new bundle.

Restart the OperatorSource

The OperatorSource reads the list of Operators in the configured Quay.io account on startup. After uploading a new Operator or a new version of a CSV file, you'll need to restart the OperatorSource pod to pick up the changes.

The pod's name begins with the same name as the OperatorSource. Using the example OperatorSource from the previous section, with "jdob" as the Quay.io username, the following demonstrates how to restart the OperatorSource:

```
$ kubectl get pods -n marketplace
NAME                                       READY   STATUS    RESTARTS   AGE
jdob-operators-5969c68d68-vfff6            1/1     Running   0          34s
marketplace-operator-bb555bb7f-sxj7d       1/1     Running   0          102m
upstream-community-operators-588bf67cfc    1/1     Running   0          101m

$ kubectl delete pod jdob-operators-5969c68d68-vfff6 -n marketplace
pod "jdob-operators-5969c68d68-vfff6" deleted

$ kubectl get pods -n marketplace
NAME                                       READY   STATUS    RESTARTS   AGE
jdob-operators-5969c68d68-6w8tm            1/1     Running   0          12s    ❶
marketplace-operator-bb555bb7f-sxj7d       1/1     Running   0          102m
upstream-community-operators-588bf67cfc    1/1     Running   0          102m
```

❶ The newly started pod name suffix differs from the original pod, confirming that a new pod has been created.

At any point, you can query the OperatorSource to see a list of its known Operators:

```
$ OP_SRC_NAME=jdob-operators
$ kubectl get opsrc $OP_SRC_NAME \
-o=custom-columns=NAME:.metadata.name,PACKAGES:.status.packages \
-n marketplace
NAME             PACKAGES
jdob-operators   visitors-operator
```

Installing the Operator Through OLM

After you've configured the Marketplace Operator to retrieve your bundle, test it by creating a subscription to one of its supported channels. OLM reacts to the subscription and installs the corresponding Operator.

Create the OperatorGroup

You'll need an OperatorGroup to denote which namespaces the Operator should watch. It must exist in the namespace where you want to deploy the Operator. For simplicity while testing, the example OperatorGroup defined here deploys the Operator into the existing marketplace namespace:

```
apiVersion: operators.coreos.com/v1alpha2
kind: OperatorGroup
metadata:
  name: book-operatorgroup
  namespace: marketplace
spec:
  targetNamespaces:
  - marketplace
```

Like with other Kubernetes resources, use the kubectl apply command to create the OperatorGroup:

```
$ kubectl apply -f operator-group.yaml
operatorgroup.operators.coreos.com/book-operatorgroup created
```

Create the subscription

A subscription links the previous steps together by selecting an Operator and one of its channels. OLM uses this information to start the corresponding Operator pod.

The following example creates a new subscription to the stable channel for the Visitors Site Operator:

```
apiVersion: operators.coreos.com/v1alpha1
kind: Subscription
metadata:
  name: book-sub
  namespace: marketplace    ❶
spec:
  channel: stable    ❷
  name: visitors-operator
  source: jdob-operators    ❸
  sourceNamespace: marketplace    ❹
```

❶ Indicates the namespace the subscription will be created in.

❷ Selects one of the channels defined in the package manifest.

❸ Identifies which OperatorSource to look at for the corresponding Operator and channel.

❹ Specifies the OperatorSource's namespace.

Create the subscription using the `apply` command:

```
$ kubectl apply -f subscription.yaml
subscription.operators.coreos.com/book-sub created
```

OLM will be notified of the new subscription and will start the Operator pod in the marketplace namespace:

```
$ kubectl get pods -n marketplace
NAME                                    READY   STATUS    RESTARTS   AGE
jdob-operators-5969c68d68-6w8tm         1/1     Running   0          143m
visitors-operator-86cb966f59-l5bkg      1/1     Running   0          12s
```

 We have truncated the output here for readability; your results may vary slightly.

Testing the Running Operator

Once OLM has started the Operator, you can test it by creating a custom resource of the same type that the Operator owns. Refer to Chapters 6 and 7 for more information about testing a running Operator.

Visitors Site Operator Example

You can find the OLM bundle files for the Visitors Site Operator in the book's GitHub repository (*https://github.com/kubernetes-operators-book/chapters/tree/master/ch08*).

There are two directories of note:

bundle
> This directory contains the actual OLM bundle files, including the CSV, CRD, and package files. You can use the process outlined in this chapter to build and deploy the Visitors Site Operator using these files.

testing
> This directory contains the additional resources required to deploy an Operator from OLM. These include the OperatorSource, OperatorGroup, subscription, and a sample custom resource to test the Operator.

Readers are welcome to submit feedback, issues, and questions on these files through the Issues tab in GitHub.

Summary

As with any piece of software, managing installation and upgrades is critical for Operators. Operator Lifecycle Manager fills this role, giving you a mechanism for discovering Operators, handling updates, and ensuring stability.

Resources

- OLM installation (*https://oreil.ly/cu1IP*)
- OLM repository (*https://oreil.ly/1IN19*)
- Marketplace Operator repository (*https://oreil.ly/VVvFM*)
- Operator Courier repository (*https://oreil.ly/d6XdP*)

CHAPTER 9

Operator Philosophy

We've noted the problems Operators aim to solve, and you've stepped through detailed examples of how to build Operators with the SDK. You've also seen how to distribute Operators in a coherent way with OLM. Let's try to connect those tactics to the strategic ideas that underpin them to understand an existential question: what are Operators for?

The Operator concept descends from Site Reliability Engineering (SRE). Back in Chapter 1, we talked about Operators as software SREs. Let's review some key SRE tenets to understand how Operators apply them.

SRE for Every Application

SRE began at Google in response to the challenges of running large systems with ever-increasing numbers of users and features. A key SRE objective is allowing services to grow without forcing the teams that run them to grow in direct proportion. To run systems at dramatic scale without a team of dramatic size, SREs write code to handle deployment, operations, and maintenance tasks. SREs create software that runs other software, keeps it running, and manages it over time. SRE is a wider set of management and engineering techniques with automation as a central principle. You may have heard its goal referred to by different names, like "autonomous" or "self-driving" software. In the Operator Maturity Model we introduced in Figure 4-1, we call it "Auto Pilot."

Operators and the Operator Framework make it easier to implement this kind of automation for applications that run on Kubernetes. Kubernetes orchestrates service deployments, making some of the work of horizontal scaling or failure recovery automatic for stateless applications. It represents distributed system resources as API abstractions. Using Operators, developers can extend those practices to complex applications.

The well-known "SRE book" *Site Reliability Engineering* (O'Reilly), by Betsy Beyer et al. (eds.), is the authoritative guide to SRE principles. Google engineer Carla Geisser's comments in it typify the automation element of SRE: "If a human operator needs to touch your system during normal operations, you have a bug."[1] SREs write code to fix those bugs. Operators are a logical place to program those fixes for a broad class of applications on Kubernetes. An Operator reduces human intervention bugs by automating the regular chores that keep its application running.

Toil Not, Neither Spin

SRE tries to reduce toil by creating software to perform the tasks required to operate a system. *Toil* is defined in this context as work that is "automatable, tactical, devoid of enduring value, and that scales linearly as a service grows."[2]

Automatable: Work Your Computer Would Like

Work is automatable if a machine could do it. If a task needs the discernment of human judgment, a machine can't do it. For example, expense reports are subjected to a variety of machine-driven boundary checking, but usually some final human review is required—of items the automated process flagged as out of bounds, if not of every receipt. The approval of reports within bounds may be automatable; the final acceptance or rejection of out-of-bounds cases may not. Work that could be automated by software should be automated by software if it is also repetitive. The cost of building software to perform a repetitive task can be amortized over a lifetime of repetitions.

Running in Place: Work of No Enduring Value

It can be uncomfortable to think of some work as having no value, but in SRE terms, work is "devoid of enduring value" if doing the work doesn't change the service. Backing up a database server is one example. The database doesn't go faster, serve more requests, or become inherently more reliable when you back it up. It also doesn't stop working. Yet despite having no enduring value, backups are clearly worth doing. This kind of work often makes a good job for an Operator.

---

1 Beyer et al. (eds.), *Site Reliability Engineering*, 119.

2 Beyer et al. (eds.), *Site Reliability Engineering*, 120.

Growing Pains: Work That Expands with the System

You might design a service so that it scales in the horizontal plane, to serve more requests or run more instances of the service. But if adding a new instance requires an engineer to configure computers and wire them to a network, scaling the service is anything but automatic. In the worst cases of this kind of toil, ops work might scale linearly with your service. Every 10% of service growth—10% more users, 10% more requests per second, or a new feature that uses 10% more CPU—means 10% more custodial labor.

Manual scaling: Just like in the bad old days

Imagine running the stateless web server from Chapter 1. You deploy three instances on three VMs. To add more web server capacity, you spin up new VMs, assign them (unique) IP addresses, and assign (per-IP) ports where the web server binaries listen. Next, you inform the load balancer of the new endpoints so it can route some requests there.

As designed and provisioned, it's true that your simple stateless web server can grow with demand. It can serve more users and add more features by spreading an increasing load over multiple instances. But the team that runs the service will always have to grow along with it. This effect gets worse as the system gets larger, because adding one VM won't meaningfully increase the capacity of a thousand instances.

Automating horizontal scaling: Kubernetes replicas

If you deploy your stateless web server on Kubernetes instead, you can scale it up and down with little more than a kubectl command. This is an example of Kubernetes as an implementation of SRE's automation principles at the platform level. Kubernetes abstracts the infrastructure where the web servers run and the IP addresses and ports through which they serve connections. You don't have to configure each new web server instance when scaling up, or deliberately free IPs from your range when scaling down. You don't have to program the load balancer to deliver traffic to a new instance. Software does those chores instead.

Operators: Kubernetes Application Reliability Engineering

Operators extend Kubernetes to extend the principle of automation to complex, stateful applications running on the platform. Consider an Operator that manages an application with its own notions of clustering. When the etcd Operator replaces a failed etcd cluster member, it arranges a new pod's membership by configuring it and the existing cluster with endpoints and authentication.

If you are on a team responsible for managing internal services, Operators will enable you to capture expert procedures in software and expand the system's "normal

---

operations": that is, the set of conditions it can handle automatically. If you're developing a Kubernetes native application, an Operator lets you think about how users toil to run your app and save them the trouble. You can build Operators that not only run and upgrade an application, but respond to errors or slowing performance.

Control loops in Kubernetes watch resources and react when they don't match some desired state. Operators let you customize a control loop for resources that represent your application. The first Operator concerns are usually automatic deployment and self-service provisioning of the operand. Beyond that first level of the maturity model, an Operator should know its application's critical state and how to repair it. The Operator can then be extended to observe key application metrics and act to tune, repair, or report on them.

Managing Application State

An application often has internal state that needs to be synchronized or maintained between replicas. Once an Operator handles installation and deployment, it can move farther along the maturity model by keeping such shared state in line among a dynamic group of pods. Any application with its own concept of a cluster, such as many databases and file servers, has this kind of shared application state. It may include authentication resources, replication arrangements, or writer/reader relationships. An Operator can configure this shared state for a new replica, allowing it to expand or restore the application's cluster with new members. An Operator might rectify external resources its application requires. For example, consider manipulating an external load balancer's routing rules as replicas die and new ones replace them.

Golden Signals Sent to Software

Beyer at al. suggest monitoring the "four golden signals"[3] for the clearest immediate sense of a system's health. These characteristics of a service's basic operation are a good place to start planning what your Operator should watch. In the SRE book that popularized them, golden signals convey something about a system's state important enough to trigger a call to a human engineer.[4] When designing Operators, you should think of anything that might result in a call to a person as a bug you can fix.

Site Reliability Engineering lists the four golden signals as *latency*, *traffic*, *errors*, and *saturation*.[5] Accurate measurements of these four areas, adapted to the metrics that best represent a particular application's condition, ensure a reasonable understanding

---

3 Beyer et al. (eds.), *Site Reliability Engineering*, 139.

4 Beyer et al. (eds.), *Site Reliability Engineering*, 140.

5 Beyer et al. (eds.), *Site Reliability Engineering*, 139.

of the application's health. An Operator can monitor these signals and take application-specific actions when they depict a known condition, problem, or error. Let's take a closer look:

Latency

Latency is how long it takes to do something. It is commonly understood as the elapsed time between a request and its completion. For instance, in a network, latency is measured as the time it takes to send a packet of data between two points. An Operator might measure application-specific, internal latencies like the lag time between actions in a game client and responses in the game engine.

Traffic

Traffic measures how frequently a service is requested. HTTP requests per second is the standard measurement of web service traffic. Monitoring regimes often split this measurement between static assets and those that are dynamically generated. It makes more sense to monitor something like transactions per second for a database or file server.

Errors

Errors are failed requests, like an HTTP 500-series error. In a web service, you might have an HTTP success code but see scripting exceptions or other client-side errors on the successfully delivered page. It may also be an error to exceed some latency guarantee or performance policy, like a guarantee to respond to any request within a time limit.

Saturation

Saturation is a gauge of a service's consumption of a limited resource. These measurements focus on the most limited resources in a system, typically CPU, memory, and I/O. There are two key ideas in monitoring saturation. First, performance gets worse even before a resource is 100% utilized. For instance, some file-systems perform poorly when more than about 90% full, because the time it takes to create a file increases as available space decreases. Because of similar effects in nearly any system, saturation monitors should usually respond to a high-water mark of less than 100%. Second, measuring saturation can help you anticipate some problems before they happen. Dividing a file service's free space by the rate at which an application writes data lets your Operator estimate the time remaining until storage is full.

Operators can iterate toward running your service on auto pilot by measuring and reacting to golden signals that demand increasingly complex operations chores. Apply this analysis each time your application needs human help, and you have a basic plan for iterative development of an Operator.

Seven Habits of Highly Successful Operators

Operators grew out of work at CoreOS during 2015 and 2016. User experience with the Operators built there and continuing at Red Hat, and in the wider community, have helped refine seven guidelines set out as the concept of Kubernetes Operators solidified:[6]

1. *An Operator should run as a single Kubernetes deployment.*

   You installed the etcd Operator in Chapter 2 from one manifest, without the OLM machinery introduced in Chapter 8. While you provide a CSV and other assets to make an OLM bundle for an Operator, OLM still uses that single manifest to deploy the Operator on your behalf.

   To illustrate this, although you usually need to configure RBAC and a service account, you can add the etcd Operator to a Kubernetes cluster with a single command. It is just a deployment:

   ```
   $ kubectl create -f https://raw.githubusercontent.com/\
       kubernetes-operators-book/chapters/master/ch03/
           etcd-operator-deployment.yaml
   ```

2. *Operators should define new custom resource types on the cluster.*

   Think of the etcd examples back in Chapter 2. You created a CRD, and in it you defined a new kind of resource, the EtcdCluster. That kind represents instances of the operand, a running etcd cluster managed by the Operator. Users create new application instances by creating new custom resources of the application's kind.

3. *Operators should use appropriate Kubernetes abstractions whenever possible.*

   Don't write new code when API calls can do the same thing in a more consistent and widely tested manner. Some quite useful Operators do little more than manipulate some set of standard resources in a way that suits their application.

4. *Operator termination should not affect the operand.*

   When an Operator stops or is deleted from the cluster, the application it manages should continue to function. Return to your cluster and delete either the etcd or the Visitors Site Operator. While you won't have automatic recovery from failures, you'll still be able to use the application features of the operand in the absence of the Operator. You can visit the Visitors Site or retrieve a key-value pair from etcd even when the respective Operator isn't running.

   Note that removing a CRD does affect the operand application. In fact, deleting a CRD will in turn delete its CR instances.

---

6 Brandon Phillips, "Introducing Operators," CoreOS Blog, November 3, 2016, *https://oreil.ly/PtGuh*.

5. *An Operator should understand the resource types created by any previous versions.*

   Operators should be backward compatible with the structures of their predecessors. This places a premium on designing carefully and for simplicity, because the resources you define in version 1 will necessarily live on.

6. *An Operator should coordinate application upgrades.*

   Operators should coordinate upgrades of their operands, potentially including rolling upgrades across an application cluster and almost certainly including the ability to roll back to a previous version when there is a problem. Keeping software up to date is necessary toil, because only the latest software has the latest fixes for bugs and security vulnerabilities. Automating this upgrade toil is an ideal job for an Operator.

7. *Operators should be thoroughly tested, including chaos testing.*

   Your application and its relationship to its infrastructure constitute a complex distributed system. You're going to trust your Operator to manage that system. Chaos testing (*https://oreil.ly/K8IUR*) intentionally causes failures of system components to discover unexpected errors or degradation. It's good practice to build a test suite that subjects your Operator to simulated errors and the outright disappearance of pods, nodes, and networking to see where failures arise or cascade between components as their dependencies collapse beneath them.

Summary

Operators tend to advance through phases of maturity ranging from automatic installs, through seamless application upgrades, to a steady normal state of "auto pilot" where they react to and correct emergent issues of performance and stability in their operands. Each phase aims to end a little more human toil.

Making an Operator to distribute, deploy, and manage your application makes it easier to run it on Kubernetes and allows the application to leverage Kubernetes features. An Operator that follows the seven habits outlined here is readily deployed, and can itself be managed through its lifecycle by OLM. That Operator makes its operand easier to run, manage, and potentially to implement. By monitoring its application's golden signals, an Operator can make informed decisions and free engineers from rote operations tasks.

CHAPTER 10

Getting Involved

All of the components in the Operator Framework, including the Operator SDK, Operator Lifecycle Manager, and Operator Metering, are still in the early stages of their lifespans. There are a variety of ways to contribute to their development, ranging from something as simple as submitting a bug report to becoming an active developer.

One of the simplest ways of interacting with both users and developers of the Operator Framework is through its Special Interest Group (*https://groups.google.com/forum/#!forum/operator-framework*), or SIG. The SIG uses a mailing list to discuss topics including upcoming release information, best practices, and user questions. The SIG is free to join from their website.

For more direct interaction, the Kubernetes Slack team (*https://kubernetes.slack.com/*) is an active community of users and developers. The "kubernetes-operators" channel in particular covers topics related to this book.

The Operator Framework GitHub organization (*https://oreil.ly/8iDG1*) contains the project repositories for each of its components. There are also a variety of supplemental repositories, such as the Operator SDK Samples repository (*https://oreil.ly/CYhac*), that further help with Operator development and usage.

Feature Requests and Reporting Bugs

One of the simplest ways, albeit an extremely valuable one, of getting involved with the Operator Framework is to submit bug reports. The framework project teams use GitHub's built-in issue tracking to triage and fix outstanding issues. You can find the tracker for each specific project under the Issues tab on the GitHub project page. For example, the Operator SDK's issue tracker can be found at the Operator Framework GitHub repo (*https://oreil.ly/l6eUM*).

Additionally, the project teams use the issue tracker to track feature requests. The New Issue button prompts submitters to select between bug reports and feature requests, which are then automatically tagged appropriately. Submitting feature requests provides a wide variety of uses cases and helps drive the project direction based on community needs.

There are a few general principles[1] to keep in mind when submitting a new issue:

- *Be specific.* For bugs, provide as much information as possible about the running environment, including project versions and cluster details. When possible, include detailed reproduction steps. For feature requests, start by including the use case being addressed by the requested feature. This aids in the feature prioritization and helps the team decide if there is a better or existing way to fulfill the request.

- *Keep the scope limited to a single bug.* Multiple reports are easier to triage and track than a report of a single, multifaceted issue.

- *Try to select the applicable project.* For example, if the issue specifically applies to working with OLM, create the issue in that repository. For some bugs, it's not always possible to determine where the problem is originating from. In those cases, you can choose the most applicable project repository and let the team triage it appropriately.

- *Use an existing issue if one is found.* Use GitHub's issue tracker's search ability to see if a similar bug or feature request is found before creating a new report. Additionally, check the list of closed issues and reopen an existing bug if possible.

Contributing

Of course, if you're comfortable working with code, contributions to the source code are appreciated. There are current instructions for setting up a development environment in the developer guide (*https://oreil.ly/Gi9mA*). Be sure to review the latest contributing guidelines (*https://oreil.ly/syVVk*) before submitting any pull requests.

For reference, the repositories for the three primary Operator Framework components are as follows:

- *https://github.com/operator-framework/operator-sdk*
- *https://github.com/operator-framework/operator-lifecycle-manager*
- *https://github.com/operator-framework/operator-metering*

---

1 See example issues here (*https://oreil.ly/sU3rW*) and here (*https://oreil.ly/m81qp*).

If you're not comfortable coding, you can still contribute by updating and fleshing out the project documentation. The "kind/documentation" label for issues identifies outstanding errors and enhancement requests.

Sharing Operators

OperatorHub.io (*https://operatorhub.io*) is a hosting site for community-written Operators. The site contains Operators from a wide variety of categories, including:

- Databases
- Machine learning
- Monitoring
- Networking
- Storage
- Security

The community provides automated testing and manual vetting for Operators featured on this site. They are packaged with the necessary metadata files to be installed and managed by OLM (see Chapter 8 for more information).

You can submit Operators for inclusion in OperatorHub.io via pull requests to the Community Operators repository (*https://oreil.ly/j0rlN*). Check out this OperatorHub.io page (*https://operatorhub.io/contribute*) with the latest submission instructions, including packaging guidelines.

Additionally, OperatorHub.io provides a way to preview how your CSV file will appear once it has been accepted and is hosted on the site. This is a good way to ensure that you have entered the proper metadata fields. You can find out more on the Operator Preview page (*https://operatorhub.io/preview*).

The Awesome Operators repository (*https://oreil.ly/OClO4*) keeps an updated list of Operators that are not hosted on OperatorHub.io. While these Operators have not been vetted in the same way as those hosted on OperatorHub.io, they are all open source, with their corresponding GitHub repositories listed.

Summary

As an open source project, the Operator Framework thrives on community involvement. Every bit helps, from participating in the mailing list conversations to contributing code for bug fixes and new features. Contributing to OperatorHub.io also helps promote your Operators while growing the ecosystem of available functionality.

Running an Operator as a Deployment Inside a Cluster

Running an Operator outside of the cluster, is convenient for testing and debugging purposes, but production Operators run as Kubernetes deployments. There are a few extra steps involved for this deployment style:

1. *Build the image.* The Operator SDK's build command chains to the underlying Docker daemon to build the Operator image, and takes the full image name and version when run:

   ```
   $ operator-sdk build jdob/visitors-operator:0.1
   ```

2. *Configure the deployment.* Update the *deploy/operator.yaml* file that the SDK generates with the name of the image. The field to update is named image and can be found under:

   ```
   spec -> template -> spec -> containers
   ```

   The generated file defaults the value to REPLACE_IMAGE, which you should update to reflect the name of the image built in the previous command.

   Once built, push the image to an externally accessible repository such as Quay.io (*https://quay.io*) or Docker Hub (*https://hub.docker.com*).

3. *Deploy the CRD.* The SDK generates a skeleton CRD that will function correctly, but see Appendix B for more information on fleshing out this file:

   ```
   $ kubectl apply -f deploy/crds/*_crd.yaml
   ```

4. *Deploy the service account and role.* The SDK generates the service account and role required by the Operator. Update these to limit the permissions of the role to the minimum of what is needed for the Operator to function.

Once you have scoped the role permissions appropriately, deploy the resources into the cluster:

```
$ kubectl apply -f deploy/service_account.yaml
$ kubectl apply -f deploy/role.yaml
$ kubectl apply -f deploy/role_binding.yaml
```

> You must deploy these files in the order listed, as the role binding requires both the role and the service account to be in place.

5. *Create the Operator deployment.* The last step is to deploy the Operator itself. You can use the previously edited *operator.yaml* file to deploy the Operator image into the cluster:

```
$ kubectl apply -f deploy/operator.yaml
```

Custom Resource Validation

When adding a new API, the Operator SDK generates a skeleton custom resource definition. This skeleton is usable as is; no further changes or additions need to be made to create custom resources.

The skeleton CRD achieves this flexibility by simply defining the spec and status sections, representing the user input and custom resource state, respectively, as open-ended objects:

```
spec:
    type: object
status:
    type: object
```

The drawback to this approach is that Kubernetes isn't able to validate any of the data in either of these fields. Since Kubernetes doesn't know what values should or should not be allowed, as long as the manifest parses, the values are allowed.

To solve this problem, CRDs include support for the OpenAPI Specification (*https:// oreil.ly/bzRIu*) to describe the validation constraints of each of its fields. You'll need to manually add this validation to the CRD to describe the allowed values for both the spec and status sections.

You'll make two primary changes to the spec section of the CRD:

- Add a properties map. For each of the attributes that may be specified for custom resources of this type, add an entry to this map along with information on the parameter's type and allowed values.

- Optionally, you can add a required field listing the properties whose presence Kubernetes should enforce. Add the name of each required property as an entry in this list. If you omit any of these properties during resource creation, Kubernetes will reject the resource.

You can also flesh out the `status` section with property information following the same conventions as for `spec`; however, there is no need to add a `required` field.

 In both cases, the existing line `type: object` remains; you insert the new additions at the same level as this "type" declaration.

You can find both the `spec` and `status` fields in the following section of the CRD:

```
spec -> validation -> openAPIV3Schema -> properties
```

As an example, the additions to the VisitorsApp CRD are as follows:

```
spec:
    type: object
    properties:
        size:
            type: integer
        title:
            type: string
    required:
    - size
status:
    type: object
    properties:
        backendImage:
            type: string
        frontendImage:
            type: string
```

This snippet is only an example of what you can accomplish using OpenAPI validation. You can find detailed information on creating custom resource definitions in the Kubernetes documentation (*https://oreil.ly/FfkJe*).

Role-Based Access Control (RBAC)

When the Operator SDK generates an Operator project (regardless of whether it is a Helm, Ansible, or Go-based Operator), it creates a number of manifest files for deploying the Operator. Many of these files grant permissions to the deployed Operator to perform the various tasks it does throughout its lifetime.

The Operator SDK generates three files related to Operator permissions:

deploy/service_account.yaml
> Instead of authenticating as a user, Kubernetes provides a programmatic authentication method in the form of *service accounts*. A service account functions as the identity for the Operator pod when making requests against the Kubernetes API. This file simply defines the service account itself, and you do not need to manually edit it. More information on service accounts is available in the Kubernetes documentation (*https://oreil.ly/8oXS-*).

deploy/role.yaml
> This file creates and configures a *role* for the service account. The role dictates what permissions the service account has when interacting with the cluster APIs. The Operator SDK generates this file with extremely wide permissions that, for security reasons, you will want to edit before deploying your Operator in production. In the next section we explain more about refining the default permissions in this file.

deploy/role_binding.yaml
> This file creates a *role binding*, which maps the service account to the role. You do not need to make any changes to the generated file.

Fine-Tuning the Role

At its most basic level, a role maps resource types to the actions (known as "verbs" in the role resource terminology) a user or service account may take on resources of those types. For example, the following role grants view (but not create or delete) permissions for deployments:

```
- apiGroups: ["apps"]
  resources: ["deployments"]
  verbs: ["get", "list", "watch"]
```

Since the Operator SDK does not know the extent to which your Operator will need to interact with the cluster, the default role allows all actions on a variety of Kubernetes resource types. The following snippet, taken from an SDK-generated Operator project, illustrates this. The * wildcard allows all actions on the given resources:

```
...
- apiGroups:
  - ""
  resources:
  - pods
  - services
  - endpoints
  - persistentvolumeclaims
  - events
  - configmaps
  - secrets
  verbs:
  - '*'
- apiGroups:
  - apps
  resources:
  - deployments
  - daemonsets
  - replicasets
  - statefulsets
  verbs:
  - '*'
...
```

Not surprisingly, it is considered a bad practice to grant such open and wide-reaching permissions to a service account. The specific changes you should make vary depending on the scope and behavior of your Operator. Generally speaking, you should restrict access as much as possible while still allowing your Operator to function.

For example, the following role snippet provides the minimal functionality needed by the Visitors Site Operator:

```
...
- apiGroups:
  - ""
  resources:
  - pods
  - services
  - secrets
  verbs:
  - create
  - list
  - get
- apiGroups:
  - apps
  resources:
  - deployments
  verbs:
  - create
  - get
  - update
...
```

Full details on configuring Kubernetes roles are outside the scope of this book. You can find more information in the Kubernetes RBAC documentation (*https://oreil.ly/ osBC3*).

Index

existing chart, building Operator from, 53

Helm Operator, 51-56

    building the Operator, 51-55

    differences from Ansible Operator, 57

    fleshing out the CRD for, 55

    reviewing permissions for, 55

    running, 55

Helm project, 49

hypervisors, using with Minikube, 11

I

idempotency

    child resource creation for Operator in Go, 71

    in Operators, 75

    in Reconcile function implementations, 69

initializing the Operator, 62

install modes for Operators in CSV file, 100

InstallPlan, 83

J

Java Operator SDK, xiv

K

kind, for custom resource definitions, 50

Kopf, xiv

Kubebuilder, xiv

kubectl

    installing or updating, 11

    running Visitors Site sample application with, 47

kubectl command

    create, 15

    describe, 19, 21, 86

    patch, 24

    version, 12

Kubernetes

    API versioning conventions, 50

    custom resources, 6

    Go client API, 72

    how it works, 1

    Operators using Kubernetes abstractions where possible, 116

L

latency, 114

lifecycle manager (see Operator Lifecycle Manager)

linting OLM bundles, 106

local mode, starting an Operator in, 77

M

manifests

    CRD manifest for Go language Operator, 66

    creating etcd Operator from, 18

    deploying for Visitors Site sample application, 47

    fetching etcd Operator manifests, 14

    for deployment of backend for Visitors Site sample application, 43

    for service deployment in Visitors Site sample application, 45

    (see also service)

    installing Visitors Site application with, 41

    packagemanifests API, 82

    upgrading etcd clusters in, 24

Marketplace Operator, 102

Maturity Model, 34

metadata.deletionTimestamp field, 74

metrics aggregation, help from Operator Metering, 36

Minikube, minikube ip command, 47

MongoDB, Operators for, 8

N

namespaces, 29

    checking for deployment object in target namespace, 71

    default, for Kubernetes clusters, 17

    indicating where Operator will be running, 77

    namespace scope for Operators, 29, 63

    scoping Operators for, with OperatorGroup, 83

    that may be accessed by an Operator, 83

naming conventions, for child resources created by Operators, 75

O

oc API, 11

OpenID Connect (OIDC) providers, 30

OpenShift (see Red Hat OpenShift)

operands, 28

    Operator termination not affecting, 116

Operator Courier

    installing, 103

generated by SDK for custom resource, 54

Special Interest Group (SIG) for Operator framework, 119

stateless web server, with Kubernetes, 3

staticweb ReplicaSet (example), 27

status descriptors, for CRDs owned by Operator in OLM, 98

stopping the running Operator process, 78

storage, Operators for, 8

subscribing to Operators in OLM, 36

subscriptions, 83
  creating for Operator installed via OLM, 108
  creation of, triggering Operator installation, 87

T

targetNamespaces designation, 84

testing
  for Adapter Operators, 59
  for running Operator installed via OLM, 109
  high-level steps for Operator testing, 77

third party resources (TPRs), 10

TLS certificates, 30

toil not, neither spin philosophy, 112-113

type field
  for Ansible Operator, 56
  for Helm Operator, 53

types.go file, 65

U

upgrades, for etcd clusters, 22

Users in Kubernetes documentation, 31

V

validation of custom resources, 125-126

values.yaml file (Helm Operator), 52
  using to populate custom resource template, 54

versions
  Operator version in CSV files, 93
  versioning and updating Operators in CSV file, 100

VirtualBox, 11

Visitors Site sample application, 39-48
  accessing, 47
  frontends, 45
  installation with manifests, 41
    backend deployment, 43
    deploying MySQL instance, 41-43
    frontend deployment, 45
  overview, 39
  testing the Operator, 109
  VisitorsSite Operator, 78

W

watches, 50
  creating for Helm Operator, 55
  defining for Ansible Operator, 57, 59

WATCH_NAMESPACE variable, 63

web servers, stateless, 3

About the Authors

Jason Dobies is a developer advocate at Red Hat. Jason has worked in the software industry for close to 20 years, developing in a variety of languages, including Python, Java, and Go. In addition to his career as an engineer, he is also an adjunct professor at Villanova University, where he currently teaches software engineering and senior projects. When not sitting at a computer, Jason enjoys spending time with his wife and two children, playing video games, and working out.

Joshua Wood is a developer advocate at Red Hat who has worked throughout his career to build utility computing with open source software. He likes fast cars, slow boats, and writing short autobiographies.

Colophon

The animal on the cover of *Kubernetes Operators* is the squacco heron (*Ardeola ralloides*). Its name comes from an Italian dialect name for this bird, *sguacco*, believed to be onomatopoeia, after its call. Though the larger part of the world's population of squacco herons are resident in sub-Saharan and southern Africa and Madagascar, others migrate between Southern Europe east to Iran and south into North Africa.

The squacco heron is a small wading bird that averages 16 to 18 inches long with a 33-inch wingspan, and weighs about 11 ounces. It is pale cinnamon and ivory in color, and has yellow legs. Adults have a bright cerulean beak with a black tip, and yellow eyes. In breeding season, adults also grow a tuft of long black and white feathers at the backs of their heads, which the birds puff out during courtship displays. They build nests in large colonies in trees by waterways or among reeds.

They primarily eat insects and insect larvae, as well as small fish, amphibians, crustaceans, and mollusks. As is the strategy for many other herons, these birds stay motionless for periods of time, waiting for their prey to come close enough. Herons can correctly determine their striking angle down into the water by taking into account the light refraction created by the water's surface.

Squacco herons are also among the heron species that have been observed using insects as bait to catch larger prey. The bird does this by first killing an insect. Then, rather than eat it, the heron places this bait on the surface of the water, to draw in hungry or curious fish or frogs. If the bug drifts, the bird returns it to its original position. Scientists are still uncertain how this behavior originates, but it seems to be something juvenile birds learn by watching adults, and get better at through practice.

Though populations are declining, their current IUCN Red List status is "Least Concern." Many of the animals on O'Reilly covers are endangered; all of them are important to the world.

The cover illustration is by Karen Montgomery, based on a black and white engraving from *British Birds*. The cover fonts are Gilroy Semibold and Guardian Sans. The text font is Adobe Minion Pro; the heading font is Adobe Myriad Condensed; and the code font is Dalton Maag's Ubuntu Mono.